Work Your Way Across The USA

You Can Travel And Earn A Living Too!

Nick Russell

Publishing Partners
Boulder City, Nevada

Published by Publishing Partners
Gypsy Journal RV Travel Newspaper
1400 Colorado Street Suite C-16,
Boulder City, Nevada 89005
E-mail BookOrders@gypsyjournal.net

Printed in the United States of America

Dedicated to all of those fulltime RVers who are living the dream, and to those who are waiting by the side of the road for their time to come.

Contents

Introduction

If you have ever wanted to travel fulltime in an RV, but did not believe there was a way to earn enough money to support yourself and your family as you travel, this book is for you.

For more than two years my wife and I have made our living from our motorhome as we travel the highways and back roads of America. In that time we have met many, many fulltime RVers who have found ways to make the money they need to finance their traveling lifestyle.

Prior to becoming a fulltime RVer, I was involved in many different business ventures, as diverse as publishing, wholesale sales, the service industry, and as the owner of retail businesses. Always fascinated with the many innovative ways people have found to earn a living, I quickly began to note the ways RVers support themselves.

Soon after we began our nomadic lifestyle, I was approached by a representative of the Escapees RV Club to present a seminar on working on the road at their Spring Escapade in Lancaster, California. We had never attended an RV rally at that point, but we quickly learned that an Escapade is a gathering of thousands of RVers who come together to visit old friends and make new ones, attend classes and seminars on the RV lifestyle, and to shop the many vendors present at the larger RV rallies.

Since that first Escapees rally in California, I have presented seminars at RV rallies in other areas of the country, and am always gratified by the turnout. Obviously plenty of RVers are interested in money making opportunities that leave them free to travel and explore this great land of ours.

At my seminars, I always invite participants to share their working experiences, and the opportunity to learn from them has been as great for me as it has been for the rest of the audience. Many of the ideas for making a living on the road included in this book come from the information shared in those seminars.

No one working opportunity is right for everyone. This is not a one size fits all world. Your interests, abilities, and financial needs may be much different than those of the people in the RV parked next to you. For that reason, the information presented here covers a broad range of interests and abilities. I hope you will think of it as an "opportunity buffet", where you can browse the entire selection and find something that is just right for you. Whatever you choose, I wish you good luck and much success. I'm always interested in the ways people have found to combine work and travel. When you're out on the road working and living the fulltime lifestyle, write and let me know how you're doing.

Chapter 1

Can *You* Live The Dream?

It's a dream many people have, but don't believe will ever become a reality. It sounds too good to be true, so how can it be? Can you really travel fulltime in your RV and earn enough money to supplement your income; or even completely finance your mobile lifestyle? The answer is a resounding *YES!*

There are well over a million fulltimers living and traveling in RVs in America today. Some estimates put that number at closer to three million. Many are retirees living on fixed incomes. Thousands upon thousands of these active older citizens have discovered ways to supplement their retirement incomes. They find the added money certainly comes in handy, while the activity provides them with something to do, gives them the opportunity to meet new friends, and keeps them from getting bored. As if anyone could become bored living and traveling fulltime in an RV!

In addition to older RVers, more and more younger people are also taking to the road fulltime every year. As their children leave the nest, many baby boomers are trading their high pressure corporate lifestyles for a simpler way of life on the road. While a few of these younger fulltimers may have some income from their previous careers, many need to work as they go to be able to enjoy the freedom their new lifestyle has to offer.

Retirees and baby boomers are not the only ones enjoying the mobile lifestyle these days. Many young families are also joining this wandering population of nomads. At a Life on Wheels conference in Moscow, Idaho, we met a young couple aged 30 and 31, along with their nine year old son, who were planning to go fulltime and home school their boy as they travel.

There are many families with young children who have chosen this wonderful alternative way of living as an escape from the drugs, gang problems, and other pressures that seem to be invading every corner of America. They want to offer their children a better lifestyle and the opportunity to experience all that this wonderful country of ours has to offer.

Many of these younger families need a regular income they can depend on to meet the everyday expenses of traveling and raising children. They have discovered that no matter what your financial needs are, with a little creativity you can meet them just as easily working on the road as you can while living in a conventional house or apartment.

Working on the road can be anything from a fulltime job to a part time endeavor. It all depends on what your individual needs and interests are. Do you only need to make a couple of hundred dollars a month for walking around money? You can do it easily as you travel. Do you need to make much more to afford the payments on your motorhome or fifth wheel trailer? There are plenty of opportunities to earn as much as you want or need. It's all up to you!

Work Your Way Across The USA

Inside this book you will find information on working opportunities and small businesses you can operate full or part time as your needs, interest, and budget dictate. Some will take a bit of investment to get off the ground, though none require a huge cash outlay. Others will not demand much more than some effort on your part.

You will learn how you can put skills you may already have to work to earn money as you travel. People everywhere you go will pay you for what you know or what you can do. You may find yourself falling back on your previous work skills, or you may explore entirely new avenues. Either way, the money is there waiting for you.

The great thing about the fulltiming lifestyle and working as you go is that you have unlimited freedom. There is no boss or corporate board controlling your time, telling you when you have to work and when you can take time off. *You* decide when you work, where you work, and for how long you work.

If you like small towns, you can stop in any charming little village you come to that catches your fancy and pause a while to practice your trade or business. If you prefer the faster pace of a large city, you will find more opportunities than you can imagine.

If being in one place for a while suits you, all you have to do is find a comfortable RV park and set up housekeeping for a season or longer. If there is a bit of gypsy in your soul and you are always looking for what lies over the next hill, you have the ability to go where you want to and earn a living along the way. It is a freedom that very few people are privileged to enjoy. This book is your passport to that freedom and that lifestyle.

Work Your Way Across The USA

Along with the many ideas for earning extra income that await you inside these pages, you will also learn hints to help make whatever you choose to do a success, along with reference information to help you learn more about many of the earning opportunities that await you.

How do I know it can be done? Because I am doing it! My wife Terry and I earn our living as we travel fulltime. Our only "house" is our motorhome. From here we produce an RV travel newspaper, write and publish books on the RV lifestyle, and do several other things to make the money necessary to meet our financial needs.

I also teach classes and give seminars on working on the road at RV rallies around the country. This activity has brought me into contact with many working RVers, who have shared their experiences in earning money on the road with me. Many of the ideas presented in the pages of this book come from those RVers who are actually out there doing what they love best, enjoying the fulltimer lifestyle and supporting themselves as they travel.

While they are all wonderful, inventive people, trust me when I say that none of these RVers are any smarter or more gifted that you are. They are everyday people like yourself, who have discovered that they don't have to wait for some elusive retirement date far in the future to live their dreams of fulltime travel. They are out there doing it right now, instead of waiting for "some day."

Before we hit the road, I owned a community newspaper publishing company, and Terry ran a commercial glass shop. We both found ourselves working at least 75 hour weeks, burning out, and not enjoying life at all. We were too busy working to live.

Work Your Way Across The USA

Our days were spent earning enough money to pay for a house full of toys we never had time to enjoy. We had a four car garage full of classic cars, but there was never a free weekend to take them out for a drive. We had a huge deck built onto our house, with a sunken hot tub, but we seldom had the time or energy to enjoy it. We lived in a wonderful part of the country that offered unlimited opportunities for outdoor recreation, but we never had a few spare hours to enjoy the nearby hiking trails, fishing lakes, or ski slopes. We were too busy working.

Meanwhile, several of our friends died suddenly, all in their 40s, and all of them working at the same hectic pace that we had been doing. When we finally opened our eyes, we knew there had to be a better way. We found that better way, and you can too!

Yes, it can be done. Many of us have broken the shackles of the conventional 9 to 5 grind and set out on our own to explore this great land of ours, working as we go. We are living a lifestyle that most others can only dream about. You can do it too!

Work Your Way Across The USA

Chapter 2

First Things First

The first thing you need to do when deciding how to earn money on the road is to determine how much money you need to make. If you only require a few extra dollars a month to cover things like an occasional movie and dinner out, entrance fees to all of those interesting little museums and attractions you discover along the way, or for an occasional round of golf, you do not need (and probably do not want) to work very hard. After all, isn't the fulltime lifestyle about kicking back and enjoying this great land of ours from the comfort of your RV?

On the other hand, if you have high payments on your RV, a family to support, or are just greedy, you are going to have to apply yourself more and put in more time and effort to make enough money to cover all of your needs. Just try not to let your traveling income activities take away from all the fun and opportunities RVing has to offer. After all, if you just escaped the high pressure corporate world, why give yourself another ulcer on the road?

Whether you need to make $100 or $3,000 a month, you can do it. Like anything else in life, you get back what you put into it. Knowing what you require helps you set a goal and will go a long way toward deciding what you will be doing to earn those extra dollars.

Get yourself a legal pad, sit down with your spouse or traveling partner, and work up a realistic budget. List every expense you have or will encounter. When creating a budget, it is all too easy to overlook the little things, like cigarettes, a visit to the local bakery for a cinnamon roll and cup of coffee every morning, or having your mail forwarded to you on the road. But those little things can really add up. If you do not have a clear picture of what you are spending, you will not have any idea how much money you need to earn.

A good idea is to list every expense you incur in an average month. Get a couple of small pocket-sized note-books and scrupulously list every penny you spend.

Be fanatical about this exercise! Don't overlook the dime you put in the parking meter or the dollar you tip the waitress at lunch. To get a true picture of your spending patterns, you have to keep track of every expenditure. I suspect that you may be surprised to find how much money goes through your hands that you never realized. This may also help you exercise a little more self-discipline in managing your money, and help cut some expenses. Do not forget to include a percentage to invest or save toward the future.

We all hope we can continue traveling forever, but having something put aside for that day when we may decide to leave the road for whatever reason is always a good idea. After you have created your budget, it is a good idea to add 15% to cover the things you overlooked (and you *will* overlook something). If nothing else, this extra

Work Your Way Across The USA

buffer will come in handy when an unexpected expense comes along, such as the need to make an unplanned trip back home for a family event, unforseen equipment repairs, or entertaining the grandkids when they come to visit.

Now that your budget is finished (and you have recovered from the coronary it gave you), list all income you currently have - retirement, income from mutual funds or investments, proceeds from the sale of your home or business if you are carrying the note, and whatever other money you receive on a regular basis. From there, it is a simple matter to see where you are at currently and where you need or want to be. The difference will be the income you have to earn as you travel.

How many of these same expenses will you take on the road with you? What many new fulltimers are surprised to discover is that they do not need to make as much money as they did when they lived in a "real" house. It is amazing to realize how much money we spend on things we do not really need, and sometimes do not even want. The money is just sitting there in our pocket and we have a place to store our newfound goodies, so we buy them. Manufacturers and marketing folks have made many fortunes on these "impulse" sales.

When you are living in an RV, there is little room to keep much, so you do not buy much. We have talked to fulltimers who live on as little as $1200 a month, and live quite well, thank you. Of course, others say they need two, three, and even four times that much to make ends meet. It is all up to how you want to live. The truth is, *most people spend all they make, whatever amount that is!* This applies just as much to people living on the road in RVs as it does to people living in houses, apartments, and condominiums.

Now your job is to decide how you will go about earning the money you need to live the traveling lifestyle. Don't look so gloomy. Whoever said work can't be fun never did it from a motorhome or other type of RV. Just remember, in this new lifestyle work is a means to an end, not our purpose in life. There is no reason you cannot choose a fun business or part time job that will help make ends meet.

Many fulltimers have found that even though their previous job descriptions may have been anything from business executive to government administrator, working a few days a month in a convenience store or a fast food restaurant is a refreshing change of pace. Sure, the pay is a lot less, but so is the stress and responsibility, and you do not have to be doing this forever. Just until you have made enough money to move farther down the road, or until it's no fun anymore. Whatever you do, you will be doing it because you want to, not because you have to. That makes all of the difference in the world to many people.

Assess Your Abilities And Interests

Let's take a few moments to take inventory of your individual abilities and interests, and how they may help you make money as you travel. Do you possess a skill or craft that you can turn into dollars? Do you have a hobby that you might turn into a business? Are you talented musically or artistically? Or maybe you have always wanted to learn something like square-dance calling or locksmithing. Now is the time. There are courses offered by community colleges, trade and technical schools, along with correspondence courses that can teach you what you want to know.

You can be sure that if you have an interest, other people do too, or else they have a need that your interest can fill. And even though you may have hung up your plunger the day you retired from being a plumber and swore you would never touch a toilet again, you might find that the skills that earned you a living for so long are in great demand as you travel. Just remember, this is not a full time job any longer, it is just what you do to earn enough money to fill up the gas tank and head on down the road. The days of hectic schedules and grumpy supervisors are behind you now. You are your own boss. It does make all the difference in the world.

Get out your handy notepad again and make a list of everything you already do that can be turned into a money making enterprise. Then add any interests you might be able to make a few bucks from. You may be surprised how many ideas you come up with. You may even ask yourself why you need this book if you have all these talents. The truth is, you probably don't. But I need the money. If you did not buy this book, I might have to figure out another way to pay for *my* travels.

The Cat May Be Away, But The Rats Still Want Their Pay

Do not forget that even though you may have left the rat race behind, the rats are still there waiting for their share of your cheese. Just as you did in your old life, you will still have to pay taxes on your earnings. However, if you operate a small business, you will also have the advantage of deducting the expenses involved. Find yourself a good accountant who understands not only small business, but fulltime RVing as well.

The urge to cheat a little (or a lot) along the way may hit some readers. Experienced working RVers say it is not worth the risk. Most use an experienced tax accountant to take advantage of every deduction the law allows, and grit their teeth and pay what they owe come tax time. Only your own basic honesty (and fear of the IRS) will determine if you do or not. I cannot make that choice for you. However, I will promise to send postcards from the road while you're in the lockup if you *do* cheat and get caught.

Remember the first rule when it comes to taxes is that to *avoid* paying taxes is legal, but to *evade* paying them is illegal. As fulltimers, there are many ways we can cut our tax obligations drastically.

First of all, we have the freedom to choose our legal domicile. Just because you grew up in Grapevine, Iowa does not mean you have to remain a legal resident of good old Grapevine once you hit the road. Did you know that the same RV that costs nearly $2,000 to register and license in California or Arizona can be registered in North Dakota or Texas for around $100?

You can choose a state with no income tax or sales tax as your legal residence. By cutting out state income taxes or expensive vehicle registrations, you can literally save thousands of dollars a year. Do your homework and make the decision that is best for you.

Type Of Business

If you decide to open your own traveling business, you will need to decide what form your business will take. There are three basic business operations; sole proprietorship, partnership, and corporation, and some variations on each. All have certain advantages and disadvantages which we will explore briefly.

1) Sole Proprietorship - This is the simplest form of business. You obtain whatever license may be required and begin operation. You have no one to answer to for your business decisions. When and if the time comes to retire, close up shop, or sell out, you can do so with a minimum of effort. One of the biggest drawbacks to a sole proprietorship is that you are personally responsible for all liabilities incurred by the business. If someone is injured by a product you sell, any awards made to the victim by a court could cost you everything you own.

2) Partnership - A partnership is a lot like a marriage. Some are made in heaven, while some are a living hell. A partnership offers the advantage of the financial reserves of two or more parties, as well as help in the day to day operation of the business. As the saying goes, two heads are better than one.

However, if both parties need to live off the business, it can severely tax the cash flow. As partners, you are liable for mistakes or expenses your partner may incur. Like marriages, partnerships often go sour. Partners may disagree on how to run the business, what form growth should take, and hundreds of other details. This friction can lead to serious problems among even the best of friends. Having been in a business partnership that went sour, I personally would never do it again. But that is my own experience. Many partnerships thrive and do very well. You have to assess your own situation and decide if the benefits outweigh the potential drawbacks.

3) Corporation - The corporation is the most complex business form, but provides the best protection for the small business owner. In the eyes of the law the corporation is a separate entity. Therefore the corporation alone assumes any liabilities incurred. In the event of a judgement this corporate shield can preserve your personal assets.

Chapter 3

Whistle While You Work

Inflation or recession, no matter what the economists say, there is always work available for those who are willing to work.

Small businesses are always on the lookout for reliable hard workers. Though it may be a little more difficult to get some jobs if the personnel manager knows you will be gone in just a matter of days or weeks, many times businesses just need someone to fill in while a regular employee is on vacation or to help them through a busy period. If you have any special skills, such as typing or word processing, you may find employers welcoming you with open arms, even though they know your employment will only be temporary.

Larger businesses, such as big department stores, may only need someone for special occasions, such as the Christmas rush or during inventory. You can find many such jobs by watching for signs in the windows of businesses, by reading the Help Wanted listings in the local newspapers, or by paying a visit to a local state employment agency. And don't overlook the value of a face to face visit. Just drop into a business and offer your services. Even if the manager or owner can't use you, if you present yourself right and can convince them of what a wonderful employee you would make, they might be able to point you in the direction of a job opening they know about at a nearby business.

There are also many private employment agencies that provide temporary workers to businesses. In this scenario, you would actually be an employee of the employment agency and they would handle the scheduling of your assign-ments, paying you and taking care of your withholding taxes and such.

Many skilled workers in every field from office settings to the construction trades hook up with an employment agency or network and keep as busy as they want to be. A lot of these temporary employment agencies are part of a larger nationwide group, and once you've established yourself with an office in one location, it's a simple matter for an office at your next stop to call up your records on a computer and put you to work.

If you possess certain professional skills, such as being a licensed or registered nurse, dental assistant, or physical therapist, there are nurses' registries that will place you in hospitals, nursing homes, and medical and dental offices anywhere you want to travel. Most states will require you to be licensed in that state, though some will grant reciprocal privileges in certain professions, so check out the require-ments first.

Likewise for union members in certain trades such as construction. If you belong to a union, the nearest union hall may be able to place you easily. Some construction workers, known in the trades as tramp workers, travel full time, moving from one job site to the next.

Larger cities often have day labor halls, where you can register for work. Usually this is unskilled labor and physically demanding, such as construction cleanup, unloading trucks, or helping with fruit or crop harvests. But it will help you stay in shape while you fatten your wallet.

Cashing In On Crops

Some fulltimers we have talked to have reported finding temporary work in Washington and Oregon harvesting apples. The farms offer a small wage and a free parking spot. Surely farmers in other parts of the country could use help from time to time too. If you can operate a tractor, harvester, or other farm equipment, your chances of finding work are even better. If you are physically up to the work, this type of labor might be interesting for a while and provide a change of pace for you. After all, isn't this new lifestyle about adventure and exploration?

Do You Want Fries With That?

As mentioned earlier, fast food restaurants and convenience stores are always looking for help. The pay isn't great, but neither are the responsibilities. If you were the Vice President In Charge of Widget Procurement in your corporate life, an unskilled minimum wage job may be a blow to your ego. But jobs like these are perfect for fulltime RVers - they're easy to find and they don't expect employees to stay forever. Many fast food establishments actually prefer older workers over teenagers because they know most adults have better work ethics and they can expect them to show up on time every day.

Work Your Way Across The USA

Tourist Season Brings Job Opportunities

One of the nicest things about fulltiming is that you have the opportunity to see all of the great tourist spots - the Florida Keys, the California coast, Pennsylvania's Pocono Mountains, and all of the other places people flock to.

Many fulltimers arrange their schedules to avoid the heavy tourist seasons in such places. They prefer to visit in the off season, after the kids are back in school and the crowds have gone home, and when the prices are usually much lower.

But for working fulltimers, the tourist season can be a great opportunity to earn money while the rest of the world plays. All of those sunburned vacationers in their Bermuda shorts and Hawaiian shirts place a real strain on every local business, from hamburger stands to RV parks. You'll find many of these businesses begging for help during their busy season. If you can cope with the crowds, you can pretty much have your pick of jobs, from cotton candy seller to assistant campground host. And when you're not working, slip into those Bermuda shorts and button up that Hawaiian shirt and join the fun. Just don't forget your sun screen!

Workamping

Workamping is a term created to describe RVers who work in exchange for a free RV site and often a small salary. Many workampers find opportunities at private RV parks where they help the owners do everything from checking in new guests, to maintenance, to helping with improvement projects. Other workampers volunteer at state and national parks, historic sites, and Corps of Engineer lakes.

Work Your Way Across The USA

We have met workampers from coast to coast and border to border. Some RVers do their workamping on a volunteer basis, happy to trade a couple of days work every week for a full hookup RV space.

On the Washington coast one summer, we ran into a couple workamping at a historic lighthouse. The wife collected admissions downstairs, while the husband led tours through the lighthouse, telling visitors about the lighthouse's history and construction. In exchange for their efforts three days a week, they received an RV site for the summer.

In Texas, we met a workamper who was volunteering at the Visitor Center at the LBJ Ranch, helping visitors learn about the former president. In Jacksonville, Florida, another fulltimer was volunteering at an old French fort that is now a National Historic Site in exchange for her RV space. Others we have met have volunteered at state parks in Texas and Washington. While these volunteers are not working for actual pay, they find that the money they save by having a free RV site is fair compensation for their efforts, and they enjoy what they are doing.

Other workampers, who find work at commercial RV parks and resorts, put in more time, but also receive a salary in addition to their parking space. This can work out very well, or turn into a losing proposition, depending upon the RV park. We have talked to workampers who were trading forty hours each (husband and wife) for a total of eighty hours, in exchange for a full hookup site.

Obviously, they could do better. They are putting in far too many hours for what they are getting in return. If they paid for their site and got minimum wage jobs at a local fast food joint, they would be money ahead. Most RV park owners who employ workampers are fair in the compensation they offer. But a few seem to think nothing of taking advantage of RVers, expecting a lot more in return than their site is worth. When workampers agree to such a situation, they are not only underselling their own labor, they are making it difficult for working RVers who come after them to negotiate a fair wage.

I always suggest that fulltimers who do not need the money and are only looking for something to occupy their time look into volunteer workamper positions at the many local, state, and national public parks and Corps of Engineer campgrounds that are always in need of help. This allows them to contribute to society, keep busy, and opens up worker slots at commercial parks for RVers who are trying to earn a living or supplement their incomes.

RV parks are not the only places workampers find jobs. Dude ranches, theme parks, private farms and ranches, summer camps for kids, and marinas have all been known to welcome workampers.

We visited a ghost town in New Mexico once that is privately owned. The owners, who have been busy restoring the town for years, told us they would love to find a workamping couple to stay at the town a few weeks while they took a vacation. The only duties would be feeding a few animals and keeping an eye out for vandals. In Arizona, a gun club was advertising for an RVing couple to spend the winter parked at their shooting range to discourage trespassers. Workamping opportunities can be just as varied and creative as workampers themselves.

Workamper News is a great publication devoted to the topic and offering job listings from RV parks and resorts around the country who are looking for campground hosts or other helpers. The majority of RV parks that advertise in *Workamper News* offer a small wage and a free parking space with hookups for your RV.

Anyone considering working as they travel should consider workamping, not only to earn money, but to save money as they go. To get a subscription to *Workamper News* write: *Workamper News*, 201 Hiram Rd., Heber Springs, Arkansas, 72543. Their telephone number is (501)362-2637. *Workamper News* is also a great source for books on RVing and the fulltiming lifestyle.

Workers On Wheels

Another resource no working fulltime RVer can do without is Workers On Wheels (WOW). This fascinating website is filled with ideas, stories from those who are making a living on the road, job listings, and a lot of other very valuable information. You can also order some very useful books and publications from the Workers on Wheels website.

Since the website is constantly being updated with new information, I make it a point to log onto it frequently, and always find news and information I can use. Their website on the Internet is www.workersonwheels.com, where you can see a sample of what Workers On Wheels has to offer.

Coleen Sykora, who edits Workers on Wheels, as well as another great RV website called RV Life and Travel (www.rvlifeandtravel.com) is herself a working fulltime RVer. As they say, she's walked the walk and talks the talk.

As we have learned, many state and national parks have

opportunities for workampers to serve as campground hosts, interpreters, and in many other positions. For information on these types of opportunities, contact the state parks department in the state you would like to work, or the National Parks Service in Washington, D.C.

Chapter 4

Selling Your Way To Success

Forget the stereotype of the traveling salesman - the huckster who makes his way across the country cheating people in small towns by day and romancing the farmer's daughter by night. The electronic age has changed the world and most small town folks these days are no more gullible than people living in big cities. As for the farmer's daughter, she took a Judo class at the community college - one false move and you're roadkill, buster!

But, if you have a good personality, and you are comfortable talking to people and you are willing to make the effort, there are plenty of opportunities to make a living or supplement your income through sales. Many husbands and wives team up to present their products and have a great time working together as they travel.

Lots of companies will pay you to represent their products as you travel, either as a commissioned salesperson or as an independent representative. There are fulltimers who sell everything from encyclopedias to vacuum cleaners, RV products, advertising specialties and even campground memberships. Go to any Samboree, Escapade or other large gathering of RVers and you'll find vendors offering all sorts of goodies for sale.

One salesman I met in Arizona represents a wholesale company that supplies gun shops and sporting goods stores. He travels throughout the Southwest, calling on a regular list of accounts. The stores place their orders through him from the huge wholesale catalogue he carries, as well as calling in orders from direct mail pieces the company provides. He makes a commission on every sale, whether he takes it himself or it comes in from a mailing piece.

While this type of selling may restrict your travels somewhat if the company assigns you a territory with a regular list of clients to contact, other companies give their representatives the freedom to go wherever they wish to drum up business. Let's look at just a few of the products you might wish to represent on the road.

Advertising Specialties

Look around you. Somewhere in your home or RV you have a pen, key ring or calendar imprinted with the name of some business. Probably many such items. Businesses use advertising specialty items imprinted with their name and message as selling tools and as thank you gifts to their customers. Someone sold those businesses all those pens, key rings and calendars, along with imprinted coffee mugs, bumper stickers, decals and much more. Every business can use advertising specialties, so the entire free enterprise system is your selling field.

Car dealers purchase imprinted license plate frames

and stickers to go on the vehicles they sell; restaurants and taverns go through thousands of imprinted matchbooks; insurance offices love to send out calendars every year... the list is endless, as are the many offerings from the advertising specialty companies.

Advertising specialty sales reps are usually self-employed and represent one or more companies. The manufacturers provide you with samples and catalogues (you may have to pay a deposit on them), you show your wares to business owners and take the order and usually a deposit, which is your commission. The order is then forwarded to the company and the specialty items are imprinted and drop shipped to the customer COD. The manufacturer collects the balance due as their part and everyone is happy.

Advertising specialties are a good line for the fulltime RVer since the sales are usually high profit and the samples and catalogues don't take up much space and are not terribly heavy to carry around the country. There is no town in this country where an advertising specialty sales rep can't make a sale. Every business you encounter is a potential customer, from the gas station where you filled your tank this morning to the coffee shop where you had lunch and the RV park where you'll spend the night. You may want to build up a regular clientele and call back on them regularly to replace items as they're given away, or you may decide to solicit new customers in every new town you come to.

One of the biggest advertising specialty companies is the Newton Manufacturing Company, located in Newton, Kansas. You'll find the names of other ad specialty manufacturers in ads in the backs of such magazines as *Income Opportunities* or *Home Based Business*, both available on newsstands.

Selling To Your Fellow RVers

The RVers you meet along the way could well be customers for the products you sell. Many fulltimers sell items specifically for the RV lifestyle - everything from gadgets to make camping easier and more fun, to RV parts, services tailored to RVers, to books about fulltime RVing.

Some RV parks frown upon such activity, and for good reason - most people are in the park to relax and get away from it all. Having someone pestering their guests isn't good for business. But if you're low key about what you do, you may find that you'll be left alone. Often a simple sign in the window of your RV or on the door of your tow vehicle will go unnoticed or ignored by the campground manager, but still bring you business.

Another way to sell RV related products is by taking a booth at one of the big gatherings, such as Escapades, Samborees, or Family Motor Coach Association functions. These events can have anywhere from a hundred to many thousands of RVers participating. You will have plenty of foot traffic past your table or booth and they are all fellow RVers who may need what you have to offer. Contact some of the major camping organizations and inquire about vendor opportunities.

Probably the biggest annual nationwide gathering of RV people is at Quartzite, Arizona every winter. There you will find a huge community of snowbirds and fulltimers gathered to escape the cold winter back east and up north, and a community-wide swap meet where you can find everything from rocks and minerals to car parts and yes, a multitude of RV products.

Some examples of items we have seen offered for sale at RV rallies includes solar panels, engine performance equipment, RV braking systems, fuel and oil additives, cellular telephones, satellite television equipment, engraved signs and name badges, sun screens to cover RV windows, campground memberships, and cleaning supplies. This is only a very small example of the many products you may want to consider selling to your fellow RVers.

We've met many RVers who travel the show circuit selling their wares and making a very good living in the process. You can too.

Selling To RV Parks

Many opportunities abound for fulltimers to sell specialty products to the RV parks and resorts where they stay as they travel. Many of these opportunities involve selling advertising in one form or another. This can be very hard, or very easy, depending on your sales skills and the product you are pushing.

Since advertising is an intangible, unlike advertising specialty products that the customer can actually hold in his hand, it may take extra work to close a sale. But for those who have the knack for it, there is good money to be made. Watch the advertisements in RV related magazines for companies seeking sales representatives.

Other Specialty Sales

I've seen people selling specialized products at everything from gun shows and antique car shows to swap meets across the country. At a huge car show in Arizona last year, one man was doing a booming business demonstrating (and selling) metal and chrome polishes. We will go into selling at these special events in a later chapter.

In my former life as a small town newspaper publisher, I had one regular salesman who called on me every three months or so with a huge catalogue of office supplies at discounted prices. I would place my order, give him a check, and in a few days the UPS man would deliver the items I had ordered.

There are plenty of other opportunities for selling items as you go, and we'll cover many of them in future chapters.

Chapter 5

Show Me The Money

There are literally hundreds of swap meets, gun shows, car shows, antique shows, RV shows, arts and crafts shows, and other special events held all across the country every month. If you sell a product along the road, you are sure to find unlimited selling opportunities at these shows.

In this chapter, we will explore selling at these types of locations, the opportunities they offer, and the types of products you may want to consider selling.

Swap Meets And Flea Markets

Pick a warm weekend and a town of more than a few hundred people, and you're sure to find a swap meet or flea market. Everyone loves these outdoor bazaars where they can search for bargains and find products that may not be offered anywhere else. There is no way to count the number of swap meets across the country, or the even larger number of vendors who make a very good living displaying their wares just two or three days per week.

Swap meet vendors sell everything from tools and

household goods to clothing, books, sunglasses, watches, auto parts, and just about anything in between. Whatever you could ever need or want, there's a good chance you'll find it at any decent sized swap meet.

Most traditional swap meets are held on Friday evenings, and all day Saturday and Sunday. But more and more swap meets in larger cities are moving inside or under metal covered roofs, and are open every day of the year.

Browsing the Internet will help you find any number of swap meets and flea markets across the country. If you haven't joined the information age yet, check the yellow pages of the local telephone directory and you'll most likely find a swap meet listed. If not, ask around. There's sure to be one somewhere fairly close.

If you decide to sell at swap meets, take into consideration the weight of the inventory you'll have to haul around, as well as the logistics of re-supplying on the road. Obviously Tee-shirts and baseball caps are lighter and easier to transport and ship than anvils or concrete birdbaths, though you'll see all of them offered for sale at swap meets.

There are hundreds, even thousands, of wholesalers who offer swap meet vendors everything from X-rated movies to belt buckles for resale. The American Surplus Dealers/American Merchandise Dealers (ASD/AMD) holds several huge trade shows every year in Las Vegas, San Francisco, and Atlantic City where you'll come into contact with more wholesalers than you ever thought existed, peddling everything you could ever imagine, and some you never could. The *ASD/AMD Trade News*, a monthly publication, is crammed full of advertising for swap meet merchandise. Contact ASD/AMD at 2950 31st

Work Your Way Across The USA

Street, Suite 100, Santa Monica, Ca. 90405-3037. Their toll free number is (800) 421-4511.

Wholesale sources can be found in several other publications, including:

The Buyers Guide, 6433 Topanga Canyon Boulevard. #544, Canoga Park, California, 91303. Their telephone number is 818-342-5357, while their e-mail address is buyersguide@hotmail.com.

Merchants News, P.O. Box 741124, Boynton Beach, Florida, 33474-1124, telephone 800-453-3532 .

Western Merchandiser, 24 Grassy Plain Street, Bethel, Connecticut, 06801-1725, telephone 203-748-2050, or check their website at www.wholesalecentral.com.

Wholesale Swapmeet Merchandising, 3980 Glenfeliz Boulevard, Los Angeles, California, 90039, telephone 323-663-6900.

Flea Market News, P.O. Box 652, Marion, North Carolina, 28752, telephone 828-652-4720, e-mail fleamarketnews@msn.com.

Any of these publications will provide you with plenty of choices of merchandise and wholesale sources to buy it from.

Some of the hottest things you'll find selling at swap meets include imprinted Tee-shirts, tools, craft items, military surplus items, knives, CDs and cassette tapes, firearms (selling guns comes with its own peculiar set of circumstances and problems), auto accessories, dried fruits and nuts, kitchen accessories, jewelry, novelty items, video tapes, and clothing. By doing just a little homework you'll discover plenty of merchandise to choose from for resale.

Some localities will want you to obtain a business

license to sell at swap meets, while others will leave you alone if you're not a regular. You might want to inquire ahead of time, or take your chances and hope the license inspector took the day off and went fishing. Unlike the IRS guys, the worst you'll probably have to do if you're caught selling at a swap meet without a license is buy one. However, in some areas of the country swap meets cannot even rent you a space unless you have a sales permit.

Some RVers who work swap meets travel in a motorhome and tow a pickup or van loaded with their merchandise. They establish a working relationship with their wholesalers and arrange to have their orders shipped to them on the road.

Some private mailbox establishments, as well as friendly campground managers, will be willing to accept your prepaid shipments and hold them for you if you make arrangements ahead of time.

If your travels take you near Los Angeles, San Francisco, New York City, or Chicago, you'll find many wholesalers you can visit to stock up on merchandise. Other swap meet dealers make occasional dips south to the U.S.- Mexico border to pick up merchandise at suppliers in the NAFTA Free Trade Zones.

Many RVing swap meet vendors who find a market where they are having good sales in a community they enjoy stay for an entire season. Others may stay for only a week or two before going off in search of greener pastures and new adventures. There are RVers who spend their summers working swap meets in the northern part of the country, and then migrate south following the sun to swap meets in warmer climates during the winter.

Work Your Way Across The USA

Just how much money can you make at flea markets? We've talked to several vendors who report routinely making $1,000 weekly incomes! Not bad for two or three days a week labor. Since most of this income is in cash, I cannot guarantee you how much of this income gets reported. Again, your own sense of honesty (as well as your fear of the IRS), will dictate how carefully you keep your records.

Gun Shows

While they may not be politically correct, there are several million shooters and gun enthusiasts in this country, and gun shows are held just about as often as swap meets and flea markets.

A gun show is an indoor event where shooters come together to buy and sell firearms, accessories, and related paraphernalia. Many dealers make their living moving from one gun show to another. In Tucson we ran into a senior citizen who travels around the country in her motorhome, exhibiting at 50 gun shows a year. While the cost for a table at a gun show is usually higher than space rent at the local swap meet, you're indoors out of the weather, and the people passing by your table are all interested in what you have for sale.

Be aware that selling firearms as a business requires a Federal Firearms License and possibly state licenses, depending on location. There are severe penalties for those who break federal firearms laws. That said, there are still lots of opportunities to make a very good living selling at gun shows.

Gun show dealers offer caps and shirts imprinted with the brand names of gun manufacturers, holsters, knives, scopes and other accessories. Some do very well selling gun related books, while others specialize in equipment for reloading ammunition.

At almost every gun show I've ever attended, someone was selling jewelry (How else are you going to keep the little woman from using that new shotgun on you when you come home from the gun show if you don't bribe her?) and doing very well at it.

Gun shows are year round events and are held all across the country. *Gun/Knife Show Calendar* is a quarterly pub-lication listing gun shows in towns and cities across the county. Here you'll find hundreds of shows listed. No matter where your travels take you, you can probably find a show listed in that area. To subscribe, call 800-258-0929.

Shotgun News, P.O. Box 56266, Boulder, Co., 80323-6266 also carries listings for gun shows, as well as ads for guns and related accessories. You'll also find lots of gun show listings by searching the Internet.

Car Shows

While not held quite as frequently as gun shows or swap meets, collector car shows are regular events in good weather. If you enjoy old cars and the people who love them, you might want to consider selling car related products.

You could make good money selling quality waxes and polishes, posters, imprinted shirts and caps, the chrome goodies gearheads love to dress up their cars with, refrigerator magnets with pictures of collector cars, key chains - you name it, if it's automotive related you can sell it at car shows. Again, the opportunities are unlimited for the savvy fulltimer.

Antique Shows

If things from days gone by are your interest, you can make a living selling at antique shows as you travel. One word of caution here - if you are going to sell antiques, consider smaller items like hat pins, chamber pots, or campaign buttons. Load on too many old roll-top desks and rocking chairs and you're liable to give your vehicle a hernia.

Many dealers do very well buying items in one part of the country where the prices are lower and transporting them to another for resale at a nice profit.

Craft Shows And Festivals

People attending craft shows and festivals are great sales opportunities. They're having a good time and their pockets are usually full of money. Every small town and big city has its own craft festival, sometimes many in a given year. I used to accuse the Chamber of Commerce in my old hometown of being a Chamber of Festivals, since they held so many events each year.

There's no getting around the fact that a lot of money changes hands at these kinds of events. I've seen (and bought) everything from small blown glass animals to leather belts, whirligigs, and paintings. If you have a talent for creating things, you could make a lot of money at craft shows.

One fulltimer who used to spend summers in our resort community made beautiful wooden address signs with a router, and he always had a line of people in front of his booth at every festival. Another vendor traveled around the state selling kettle korn, popcorn popped on-sight in a huge iron kettle. And what's a festival without face painting? Decorate children's faces with washable paint and you'd be surprised how much money you'll make.

Booth space at festivals can be much more expensive than at swap meets and other events, so do your arithmetic and be sure you can make enough of a profit to make it worth your time.

Just as at swap meets, gun shows, antiques shows, and car shows, do your homework to discover the right products and you can make a very good living working the craft show and festival circuit.

The secret to getting into selling at swap meets and other shows and festivals is to attend several in different parts of the country as you travel. Talk to the vendors and learn what is selling. This is one of the most popular methods of earning money as you travel. You usually only display two or three days a week, leaving you plenty of time to get to the next event and explore the countryside along the way.

Chapter 6

Put Your Talents To Work

What's your special talent? Are you an artist? A musician? Do you bake the world's best cinnamon rolls? Whatever your special talents, there's bound to be a way to turn them into money on the road.

Drawing On A Whole New Income

For those blessed with artistic talent, it may be possible to make money through any number of avenues - selling your works at arts and craft shows, through galleries, or directly to consumers. Maybe the RV park where you are staying is in a beautiful setting and the owners would love to have a gorgeous painting of the premises hanging in the office.

If pen and ink is your specialty, fellow RVers might want to buy a small portrait of themselves, or a sketch of local areas of interest. You might duplicate local scenes on notepads for sale at area shops. For years I had a caricature drawing of myself at work at my typewriter hanging in my office at the newspaper. As I recall, the work was done by a young man at a craft festival. It was well worth the $15 or so I paid him for it.

Say Cheese

Everyone claims they hate having their picture taken, but we all secretly love it. If you're an accomplished shutterbug, you may be able to earn traveling money doing portraits, shooting weddings or even taking photos for the campgrounds where you stay. We once drove our classic Corvette on the Arizona Old Route 66 Fun Run, a gathering of hundreds of classic cars for a fun-filled two day cruise down the Mother Road. One enterprising photographer stationed himself along the route and shot photos of the cars as they passed. The next day he was doing a booming business selling color prints of the cars to their owners as a memento of the event. Why wouldn't the same thing work at a Samboree or other major gathering of RVers? I've heard of photographers who make money shooting portraits of pets. If you're smart enough to operate a 35mm camera, you're smart enough to figure out a way to make a buck at it.

A Couple Of Offbeat Ways To Use Your Artistic Talent

Who says a true artist must suffer? That doesn't sound like any fun at all! Just because you have artistic talent doesn't mean you can't have fun with it. Why not consider painting murals on the sides or backs of RVs? Or maybe creating personalized spare tire covers for fellow RVers? Everyone wants a way to set their rig apart from the rest of the world, and they could pay well for your personalized touch. I recently heard of a lady who specializes in painting portraits from photographs. She sets up her easel under the awning of her RV and begins to paint. Before too long, she attracts a few visitors, who quite often hire her to create a portrait for them. Quite often, the customers are so pleased with the result that they send her photos of their grandchildren to be painted.

Music To Your Ears

You don't have to be able to put on a Las Vegas style performance to earn money as an entertainer. Many musicians pick up extra money as they travel by performing in local nightspots, at gatherings in RV parks, and even at fairs and festivals.

We spent a good bit of an afternoon once enjoying a one-man-band performer at a festival. The musician played drums, harmonica, cymbals, and other assorted instruments at the same time, and judging by the tips he was receiving, we weren't the only ones who appreciated his efforts. Another performer made quite a bit of money strolling through the fair in full kilt playing bagpipes. At an RV gathering in Moscow, Idaho, we were entertained by Terry Raff, a singing mountain man and cowboy poet who spends part of each year traveling from RV park to RV park performing and selling tapes and CDs of his music. We know other performers who travel from RV park to RV park entertaining, especially in the South and Southwest during snowbird season.

No musical talent, but love music? You might consider putting together a good assortment of CDs and some decent equipment and hiring out as a DJ for dances, weddings and parties along your route. It would be best to have an assortment of music, from oldies to country to contemporary to be able to play different gigs and serve people with different musical tastes.

Just Clowning Around

They say all the world loves a clown, and I know I do. It doesn't take any special training to perform as a clown, just a wild costume and the personality to go with it. Clowns are in demand to perform at childrens hospitals, birthday parties and other events. RV parks might well hire a clown to entertain at some of their events. So grab your big red rubber nose, slip into your huge shoes and go make somebody smile. You can smile later as you count your money.

Tell Me A Story

Over the years I've encountered several professional storytellers - people who get paid to tell stories in libraries, schools and to different groups. One popular storyteller I met in Tucson, who specializes in tales of the Old West, keeps busy traveling to dude ranches, campgrounds, schools and festivals, where people sit in rapt attention as his beautiful, melodious voice takes them back to the wild days of outlaws and Indians. If your "the one that got away story" is the delight of your fishing buddies, you might just have what it takes to become a professional storyteller.

I Just Love Your Buns

If you have Grandma's secret recipe for cinnamon rolls, peanut brittle or fudge, you just might find you're too busy in the kitchen to get outside and see much if you're not careful! Whip up a batch of your goodies, open the windows of your RV to let those delightful aromas lure in the customers and you just might be surprised how much "dough" you make.

No matter what it is you do, there's a good bet someone is willing to pay you to do it. Take a moment to consider what special talents you have and see if you can't put them to work to finance all or part of your travels.

Work Your Way Across The USA

Chapter 7

Skills That Will Pay The Way

Just because you may be retired doesn't mean you can't use your skills to make money. Everywhere you travel, you will find opportunities to earn a living using your professional skills. Again, remember that this is all about making money to enjoy life on. Just because it's work doesn't mean it has to be a job!

Take A Little Off The Top

I'm always depressed that I followed in the family tradition and went bald while I was in my early twenties. Not nearly as depressed as my sister - she really had a hard time getting a date! Still, it's unfair that I've spent years getting the top of my head sunburned while men old enough to be my grandfather still boast full heads of hair. But my loss can be your gain if you have barbering skills. More than one trained barber (and quite a few amateurs) pick up extra money cutting hair in RV parks. Fellow campers usually know the value of a dollar and will patronize you instead of those high-priced places in town where they don't have barbers, just some silly guy named Dwayne who calls himself a "hair stylist."

Yes, there are probably laws in most states against practicing barbering without a license, and some RV park managers might frown on it. But if you keep things low key, you can probably get away with it. If you do get caught, tell that tax cheater in the next cell to share my postcards with you. Us fulltimers have to stick together.

Make Me Beautiful

Likewise, women on the road will miss their favorite hairdresser and want someone they can relate to and have something in common with. Who better than a fellow RVer? If you're a beautician, you will have ladies flocking to your RV once the word gets out. Can you do nails? Even more chance to make a little extra "scratch." The same rules of caution mentioned above apply as to licensing - these days I think they have co-ed dorms in jail.

Mr. Fix-It

God apparently figured that as long as he was withholding height and hair from me, he might as well give any mechanical ability I should have to the next guy too. While some people can rebuild the starboard engine on the Queen Mary with a crescent wrench and a Phillips screwdriver, I have to pay someone to attach the license plates to my rig.

If you can wield a wrench, understand the workings of an electrical system or figure out why a toilet doesn't flush, you'll find more work than you want along the road. RV park managers will happily pay you to fix things around the place, fellow RVers will call on you to help them solve mechanical problems with their outfits, and every local bulletin board will provide you with the opportunity to let the world know you're in town and available. In most areas a reliable handyman or mechanic is hard to find and usually booked up for weeks. You can take on the overflow the locals can't get to, and take a nice chunk of change with you when you leave.

The Sound Of Music

Recently I heard of a gypsy piano tuner who makes his living traveling from town to town adjusting and tuning pianos for private musicians, schools, and churches. Over time, he's established a regular route of customers, and his business has spread by word of mouth. This RVer is legally blind, and his wife drives their motorhome. If you have the ability to tune or maintain musical instruments, you could turn music notes into bank notes.

Sewing Up Profits

God blessed me with incredible good looks and a real talent for stretching the truth. In turn he shorted me (no pun intended) in the leg department. My tiny little legs barely reach the ground. Since it's rather hard to find pants in my size (dwarf portly) in most stores, I have to have everything hemmed. More than one seamstress has put some of my money into her vacation fund in exchange for a couple of hours with needle and thread. If you can sew a straight seam, you might well be able to pick up some walking around money.

See, I Just Dropped This Cigarette ...

Smoking's a bad habit. It costs a fortune, it makes your breath smell so bad that even my bald sister won't date you, and sooner or later you burn something.

It happens. A carelessly handled cigarette. A dropped steak knife. Something gets snagged when you're loading the RV. The dog or cat gets mad because you left it in the RV while you went on a tour of the Apple Blossom Hall of Fame and worked out their boredom on your sofa. The result is an ugly hole in the upholstery. Several people make a little (or a lot) of money repairing those unsightly rips and tears. It doesn't take much but a little talent and a lot of patience, and the rewards can be very lucrative.

I Can See Clearly Now

Before she threw away her former life and ran away with me to become a gypsy, my wife spent years in the glass business. More than one burly trucker was put in his place when "that little gal" climbed up on the hood of his rig and repaired a chip before it spread into a spider web of cracks. Windshield repair doesn't take a lot of equipment, and anyone with a little bit of mechanical ability can learn how to do it. Remember, you live among RVers - people who spend much of their time on the road dodging flying rocks and cinders. I'll bet a stroll through just about any populated RV park will find plenty of potential customers for you. When word gets around an RV park that Terry does windshield repair, we've had people come knocking on our door seeking her services.

Making Bowser Beautiful

After the cocker spaniel ruins the sofa, his owners may get smart and find a way to keep him out of trouble the next time they tour the Apple Blossom Hall Of Fame (who can see it all in one trip?). Why not take him to be groomed while the rest of the family is off having fun? Let's face it, ever since that unfortunate incident with the skunk last week, the old boy hasn't been too pleasant to be around anyway. Pet groomers can cash in on dog lovers and make a profit as they lavish attention on the family mutt. And don't forget the opportunity for pet sitting. Why not let the canine equivalent of Jaws stay in your RV and destroy your sofa the next time his owners have to leave him behind? Don't worry, word has it there's a good upholstery repairman two spaces over.

Pet grooming and sitting aren't the only ways to make pennies from pooches. If you can get inside the canine mind and understand what makes Fido tick, you might find customers who will pay you to train their animals. There is nothing more comforting than a well trained dog, and nothing more obnoxious than an out of control animal. The first can be a delight to its owners and to fellow campers. The latter will have the neighbors complaining to management and its owners finding themselves evicted in no time at all. So make everyone's life easier (and yours richer) by giving dog obedience classes.

What's Your Sign?

When I was in the newspaper business, every Christmas I paid a nice couple to decorate our office windows with holiday messages. These artists picked up a good bit of money to offset their holiday shopping expenses from decorating storefronts. And Christmas isn't the only holiday that you can make money painting windows for. Businesses need window signs for Easter, Fourth of July, Thanksgiving, etc. to advertise sales and special events - the opportunities are unlimited. Add to that painting overhead signs or signs on delivery vehicles, and you can see how many ways there are to make money painting signs.

Vinyl Repair

A simple vinyl repair kit and some practice can make you an expert at repairing rips and holes in automobile, boat, and RV seats. Again, you will find a lot of work at just about any RV park simply by hanging a sign in your windshield.

Chimney Sweep

You may think chimney sweeps have gone the way of hoop skirts and button shoes, but this skill is actually very much alive and well, and in demand. Chimney sweeps can make a very good income for a few hours of work and a lot of soot.

Grandma Goes High Tech

Remember those embroidered doilies your grand-mother had on every piece of furniture in her house? If only Grandma could see you now! At several RV rallies and specialty shows we have visited, we have run across people using computerized embroidery machines to create custom hats, shirts, and jackets with RV and club logos, as well as other artwork. These thread artists always seem busy, and sometimes have customers standing in line around their booths making selections.

The Cutting Edge

Everybody with a dull set of cutlery, pocketknife, or pair of scissors will be glad to see you if you offer professional sharpening services. This is an income opportunity that you can pursue in RV parks, at swap meets, and even at specialty shows. Having a selection of knives and sharpening equipment for sale will also help to boost your profits. While you are at it, why not call on local barber shops, restaurants, and butcher shops to offer your services? Build up a list of satisfied clients and you could easily develop a route to follow on a regular basis.

Going... Going... Gone!

Don't you just love an auction? I know I do. The excitement of the bidding, the hope of finding a hidden treasure. The chance to snoop through somebody else's belongings. Just keep your hands folded in your lap. If you wave at your buddy across the room you just may find yourself as the happy owner of a pair of matched goatskin boots. Somebody has to sell all those neat things we see at auctions. There are professional auction schools, or maybe you can practice on your own and learn to talk that fast. If so, you can earn a good living as a traveling auctioneer, selling everything from farm equipment to distressed freight to Aunt Florence's collection of salt and pepper shakers.

The Hands Of Time

In this day of $2 digital wristwatches at every truck stop and flea market you visit, there are still people who appreciate quality and will pay to own and maintain fine timepieces. If you have a mechanical mind and the patience of Job when it comes to dealing with tiny parts, you might develop a career in watch and clock repairing. In addition to people you meet in RV parks and at rallies, jewelry stores and pawn shops might pay you for your repair work. You can also make a nice profit buying broken watches at yard sales and flea markets, repairing and then reselling them.

Diamonds Are A Girl's Best Friend

Closely associated with watch repair is jewelry repair. You can make good money repairing jewelry, as well as buying old items for repair and resale. If you have an artistic side to you, you might also create your own line of jewelry. Jewelry doesn't have to be expensive to be profitable. At a Good Sam rally we attended in Michigan once, the only vendor who was doing any business was a woman with a couple of tables full of inexpensive costume jewelry. She had ladies lined up waiting to give her their money.

There's More To Routing Than Planning A Trip

Anyone who knows me is well aware that I am "tool challenged" to the point that when I tried to purchase a power saw at the hardware store in our small town once, they wanted a note from my wife before selling it to me. So when I received a Dremel rotary tool for Christmas a couple of years ago, I obediently put it away before I hurt myself. Eventually I dug it out, and was amazed at the things one can do with a Dremel tool! We even used it to cut through steel when we were building our bus conversion! I met a fellow at a swap meet once who was using a Dremel with a router attachment to make custom desktop name signs. For a little bit of work and some wood stain, he was turning old pieces of lumber into dollars.

Every fulltime RVer has some skills they picked up in their old life that they can use to finance all or part of their travels. What are yours? Why not brush up on them and get back to work?

Work Your Way Across The USA

Chapter 8

Take Advantage Of New Technology

Computers have truly revolutionized the world. They make tasks easier for those still in the working world, prolong our lives through applications in the health and medical fields, and make our world safer in so many ways. With the growth of the Internet, computers also make it easier for fulltimers to stay in contact with family and friends while on the road. More and more campgrounds are offering modem connections for RVers as they realize the advantages of, and demands for, this fast-growing technology.

Computers also provide working fulltimers with a valuable earning tool. The opportunities for making money with your computer are limited only by your imagination and your personal interests.

Word Processing And Typesetting

With the addition of a good quality laser printer to your computer workstation, you expand the possibilities for earning extra money from your electronic wizard.

Campgrounds may pay you to create brochures, fellow campers might avail themselves of your services for everything from correspondence to creating flyers for their own traveling businesses. Businesses you visit along your route may need an extra pair of hands on a keyboard during busy periods.

Creating Internet Web Pages

More and more campgrounds are getting onto the World Wide Web as computer use grows among campers. There is a lot of money to be made creating Web pages not only for RV parks, but for any number of businesses and government and social service agencies, not to mention your fellow RVers. For the sophisticated Internet user, this could be an electronic goldmine to finance your travels.

There are many good computer programs that will allow you to produce professional grade Web pages with just a little effort. I am far from computer literate, but using Front Page, I was able to create our company's website in just one evening.

Desktop Publishing

People will pay you for what you know. Proof positive is the fact that you purchased this book. (If you didn't purchase the book, you may be a shoplifter. If that's the case, sooner or later you are going to get caught and go to jail, where you belong. Don't expect me to send you any postcards from the road!)

You don't have to be an expert on any particular topic to make money in desktop publishing. A few hours spent in

Work Your Way Across The USA

a library can give you a working knowledge of many topics that you can then condense into a booklet, pamphlet, or other printed work. I have seen everything from recipe books to travel guides to local histories created with desktop publishing programs, and they all sell. So what do you know enough about, or what can a little research help you turn into a salable desktop published product?

I have created several different booklets of special interest to RVers. One is a listing of over 500 free and low cost camping places from coast to coast, another is a guide to over 250 fairgrounds where budget minded RVers can camp, a third is a listing of over 200 truck stops where RVers can plug in their laptop computers and check their e-mail from the road, and yet another is a listing of nearly 1,000 RV dump stations from coast to coast. They range from a dozen to 25 pages, and are stored in my computer's hard drive and simply printed out on my laser printer and stapled together as the orders come in. Prices on these booklets range from $6.95 to $8.95, and every month they bring in a few hundred dollars to help us move on down the road.

Except for works of fiction, there is no such thing as unique information. While you cannot legally copy the written creation of someone else and market it as your own, you can gather information from several different sources through research and repackage it in your own format.

There are literally thousands of topics you can research and turn into booklets just like these. What subjects interest you? Hiking? Fishing? Antiques? Cooking? Treasure hunting? With a few hours research, these and many more subjects can be formatted into booklets and reports for sale to others who share your interest.

From booklets and reports, it is an easy step up to writing and publishing traditional books. New technological break-throughs such as computer page layout programs and print-on-demand are making it possible for anyone to become a publisher and market their books for a very small investment. After using this technology to publish several books of my own, I am convinced it is the greatest technological advancement since the Gutenberg printing press.

Where once it required several thousand dollars to self-publish a book, now it can be done for not much more than a couple hundred bucks. Is there a best selling author lurking inside you?

We have formed a company called Publishing Partners to assist would-be authors in taking advantage of this new technology to produce and market their books, offering complete production services, from proofreading and editing to production. If you would like to see your work in print, contact us at Publishing Partners, 1400 Colorado Street, Suite C-16, Boulder City, Nevada 89005 or e-mail us at PublishBooks@aol.com

Books Without Paper?

These days, you can even become a publisher without ever touching a scrap of paper. The techno-heads tell me that the wave of the future is the e-book, a book published in electronic format and purchased online, then downloaded for reading. There are hundreds of online e-book stores where you can sell your work to the reading public.

Work Your Way Across The USA

One author claims to make up to $5,000 a month publishing and selling e-books online. There is a lot of interest in electronic publishing these days, and any good bookstore will have several titles available on the new technology.

E-books have a decided advantage over printed matter for the publisher, in that there is little or no investment in production, since you do not have to pay for printing and binding. At most, your expense is limited to the cost of a floppy disk or CD. If you distribute your product via e-mail in PDF format, you don't even have that cost.

At a recent RV rally where we had a vendor booth, we experimented by packaging the RVing booklets mentioned earlier in CD format, and were very pleased with the results. In just a few hours on the last day of the show, we sold several CDs at a very handsome markup. The experience has opened up a new product line for us.

My Grandson, The Star!

With a simple desktop publishing program, a digital camera and scanner, and some relatively inexpensive bindery equipment, you can create a line of simple customized small children's books. By writing several short stories into different books, you can set up your computer program to allow you to drop in the name and photograph of children to create their own custom book - *Johnny Goes To The Grand Canyon With Grandma and Grandpa, Susie's Special Saturday, Billy's Summer Adventure* - you get the idea. Doting grandparents will love giving these personalized gifts to the kids back home.

Teach A Class And You Might Get $$$ Instead Of Apples

Remember how intimidating your computer was the first time you sat down in front of it? Many of your fellow campers are just as confused as you once were by all the new technology. You could help them learn while you help your budget by teaching basic computer and/or Internet classes as you travel. Many of us find computer manuals, with their many pages written in Nerdeese, to be useless. To learn, we require hands on instruction. Not only will teaching computer classes make you money, you'll make some good friends in the process.

Offer Paralegal Services

There's a reason for all of those lawyer jokes. Did you know that much of the work you pay your attorney big bucks for is actually passed on to a low salaried office worker to complete? Simple things like wills and living wills, powers of attorney, lease agreements and other routine legal matters that do not involve an appearance in a court of law can be handled by a paralegal for a lot less money than a law office will charge. The forms are the same, and one does not have to be an attorney to prepare them in many states. The growing field of paralegal work has taken a lot of work away from traditional attorneys' offices and saved consumers a ton of money. Most legal forms are available on computer disk, everything is standard, and all you have to do is plug in the information your clients give you in the proper places. Be sure to check

60

the laws in the states where you want to work if you decide to operate a business as a paralegal. If there are no restrictions on doing so, you can generate a very good income.

Here's My Card

We have several little income producing endeavors going, and each one helps us buy enough fuel to get on down the road to our next adventure. Recently we picked up an inexpensive computer program that allows us to produce business cards on our computer. Fellow RVers, RV parks and small businesses will all be happy to order cards from you and save the high cost commercial printing shops charge for business cards.

Work Your Way Across The USA

Chapter 9

A Potpourri Of Money Making Ideas

There are plenty of other ways you can make money as you wander across the country. Included here are several ideas you might consider to turn a profit.

Teaching

If you know it, someone else wants to learn it too. RVers are curious people interested in all sorts of things. There is no limit to what you can teach your fellow campers, and get paid in the process. There are professional instructors who visit RV shows and events across the country teaching classes in all areas of interest.

Others operate on a smaller scale, teaching short classes at RV parks where they visit. Here are just a few ideas for classes you might be able to teach: Computer use, basic RV and auto maintenance, self-defense, treasure hunting and metal detecting, drawing and painting, photography, square dancing, playing musical instruments, cooking.... you get the idea. Now get busy and get to class!

Conducting Seminars

Closely aligned with teaching classes is conducting seminars. If you have an area of expertise, you can find a great source of income in conducting seminars. Some of the seminars I have attended or heard about: Driving motorhomes, living trusts, investing, buying distressed real estate, lowering income tax obligations, homesteading, traveling the Alaskan Highway, and various small business opportunities. People holding seminars can profit from more than one source. Some seminars are free, while others require an entrance fee, often as much as $50 or $75. At most seminars, books on the subject, many times written by the host, are for sale.

Photo Business Cards And Calendars

There are several companies around the country that create business cards and personalized calendars complete with photos of the customer's business. You can connect with one of these specialty printers and sell photo business cards to your fellow campers, as well as photo calendars to RV parks and other businesses. The same printers who can provide this service can usually also print post cards. Anyone with a decent 35mm camera and basic photography skills can do this and make money.

Rubber Stamps

A simple, inexpensive rubber stamp press and a basic selection of type styles are all you need to create personalized rubber stamps for customers. It's easy, the markup is fantastic and you can easily take orders one day, make the stamps that evening and deliver them and collect your money the next day.

Name Badges

I don't know about you, but for me senility kicked in around the age of 12. It's most apparent when it comes to remembering people's names. I can be introduced to someone and five minutes later forget their name. It can be very embarrassing. I've been married to my wife for nearly four years as of this writing, and for some reason I continue to call her father Jim, and he continues to remind me that his name is Pete. I've tried to get him to change his moniker to make my life easier, but he's so darn stubborn. That's why so many RVers wear name badges, little plastic pins with their names engraved or printed on them. Many others use name badges to signify their membership in clubs or organizations. The equipment to produce name badges isn't very expensive and even I could learn to operate it, so I know you can too. The markup is very good on these handy little items. Err.... I'm sorry, what did you say your name was?

Driving Tour Buses

You must be a good driver or you wouldn't be able to get around the country in your big RV. Have you considered driving a tour bus or van? Many National Parks, tourist areas, and resorts have guided tours of the sights available for visitors. With a good driving record, you can make money showing other folks around while you see some great places yourself. We met a couple who drive tour buses at the Grand Canyon, and they told us they each make about $16 an hour, and get a discounted RV site at the National Park. Pretty good pay, and you sure can't beat the scenery. Usually a commercial driver's license will be required, but getting one isn't a major hurdle to overcome.

Small Scale Carpenter

I met one RVer who creates custom dollhouses that are absolute works of art. His Victorian houses, with all their gingerbread trim, sell very well, and for huge sums of money. Other popular models include a log house style doll house, and one designed as a farm house. He adds to his profits by selling miniature furniture to go with his diminutive domiciles.

This Town's Not Big Enough For The Two Of Us

Admit it, there's a little bit of John Wayne in all of us who grew up watching those great old cowboys on the silver screen. We all fantasize about facing down the local gunslinger at high noon on some dusty Western street. Just as long as we're both shooting blanks. Theme parks and re-created historical areas hire lots of folks to walk around in period costumes and demonstrate old time skills to the visitors. Imagine that - getting paid to play dress up!

Lock Up Profits

Another fairly low cost business you can get into is making keys for autos, RVs and homes. A simple key making machine and a good selection of key blanks are all you need to make money at flea markets, in RV parks, at RV rallies, or wherever you go. One locksmith we know had a regular route of truck stops he would set up in. The truckers came to expect him and he made a lot of money cutting new keys for their rigs for them. Be aware that a selection of key blanks large enough to keep you in business is going to be heavy. Plan the weight into your overall load if you decide this business is for you.

Washing And Detailing RVs

Who wants their prized recreational vehicle coated with road grime? But who wants to have to clean it? You do! Many of the people who travel a lot in their RVs are either unable or disinclined to wash and wax their RVs themselves. And who can blame them - it's hard work! But with a little soap and elbow grease, you can grease the wheels to financial freedom as you travel.

Consulting

In a couple of decades in the community newspaper business, I've learned a thing or two about publishing and what makes a newspaper successful. Over the years several of my fellow publishers have paid me well to help them solve problems with their newspapers. If you have a professional specialty, you might consider working as a consultant as you travel. The returns can be very rewarding.

Organizing Caravans And Tours

RVers have all kinds of different personalities. Some are loners who enjoy discovering new places on their own. But many more would enjoy the chance to join an organized tour or caravan to some exciting destination such as Alaska,

Mexico, across Canada or even down old Route 66.

By organizing such RV tours, you can turn a very good profit while you meet new friends and see some great countryside. Income doesn't have to be limited to tour fees - campgrounds, restaurants and attractions along the way might be more than willing to make it worth your while to include a stop with them on your route.

If you don't think you have the organizational skills to run your own caravan, there are plenty of caravan companies that hire RVers to help make their trips go smoothly. They get to have some wonderful adventures with the caravan, and make money too!

Personalizing Spare Tire Covers

Who really wants a spare tire cover advertising the dealership where they purchased their RV? You already paid him too much, and now you're supposed to be a rolling billboard too? I don't think so! If you're a bit of an artist, you could make your fellow RVers very happy, and yourself a buck or two in the process, by buying up a bunch of blank spare tire covers and personalizing them with customers' names or other messages.

Pinstriping

If you've got a steady hand and an eye for graphics, there may be money waiting for you. RV owners, car enthusiasts and even car dealers pay a lot of money for custom pinstriping. I had pinstriping added to a classic Mustang I owned a while back and it cost me $100. The tape artist spent less than three hours on the job and we both parted happy.

Washing Windows

As much as your fellow RVers hate to wash their rigs, business owners and managers hate washing their big display windows. And unlike the folks parked next to you in the big diesel pusher, business people usually don't have the time for such chores anyway. All it takes is a bucket, a squeegee, some paper towels and soap and you can be in the window business. The going rate for the people who did the windows at my newspaper was $10 for a job that took them less than twenty minutes. I hate washing all the windows in my RV and don't carry a ladder to get up to them. I would gladly pay someone else to do the chore. Could that someone be you?

Yard Work

Remember all those nice little old ladies who paid you to mow their lawns back when you were in school? Have I got good news for you! You may have graduated and gone on to bigger and better things, but those lawns and a whole new crop of little old ladies are still out there waiting for you right now.

If you can fit a power mower, a couple of rakes and maybe a hedge trimmer into your truck, you can take a trip back in time, and make enough money to buy the gasoline to continue your trip down the road.

Carpet Cleaning

By now you get the idea - people will pay you to do the things they can't or don't want to do. If you're willing to lug a steam cleaner around in your travels, you could make a profit cleaning RV park facilities and the rigs of fellow travelers, as well as homes and businesses in the places you visit.

There's Gold In Them Thar Hills!

I've got a pal in Arizona who's hobby is metal detecting. After he dug up every lost coin, piece of cheap jewelry, and trinket that anyone had lost in his town during the last fifty years, he turned his efforts to prospecting. Over the years he has found several nice small nuggets, but his greatest discovery was a large, handsome nugget that paid for a new metal detector and several other toys. There is a lot more gold still undiscovered than has ever been found, and there are a lot of modern day prospectors still able to make a living if they go at it right. I know of one college graduate who paid for his education by panning gold in the California mountains every summer. Once you have some experience under your belt and have staked out some good hunting grounds, you might even consider guiding newcomers to the hobby, for a fee.

Selling CDs And Movies

Here's another great selling opportunity. RV parks and fulltimers might be willing to buy used VHS movies and music CDs. You might even think about taking the movies and CDs they currently have in trade, allowing half price or so. If nothing else, you'll have entertainment until your next customers show up. There are also wholesalers who will sell you brand new movies and CDs. Many of them advertise in the same publications where swap meet and flea market vendors find wholesale suppliers.

Racking Up Profits With Rice Bags

We shared a vendor booth at an RV show with a couple who make and sell rice bags, and were amazed at the money they were making. They purchased cloth in various patterns, sewed it into simple bags about 8 by 11 inches, and filled them with plain white rice they purchased in bulk. The bags were then sewed shut. When placed into a microwave oven for three minutes, or in a freezer, the bags offer wonderfully soothing comfort for aches and pains, and last forever. They had pennies invested in each bag, and sold them for $8 each. This is an item that would sell well at any flea market, rally, specialty show, or gathering.

Run Away To The Circus

A while back I read an article about a husband and wife fulltiming couple who joined a traveling circus as tutors and child care workers for the circus members' children. While we were camped at the Goshen County Fairgrounds in Torrington, Wyoming a traveling circus set up shop and I spent some time visiting with some of the crew. They travel in RVs, work eight months a year and have the other four months to themselves. Another couple we met worked as advance publicity staff for a circus, going into communities ahead of time to set up sponsors, sell program advertising, and select a location in which to set up the show. Can you think of anything more fun than going to the circus? Sure you can - becoming a part of the circus!

Multi-Level Marketing

Please, don't try to convince me I can get rich as an Amway distributor. I know some people do very well selling Amway and other such products, and they are indeed fine products. It's just not for me. But I know several people who swear the income potential in the multi level marketing plans they are involved in is unlimited. Many of the established multi level marketing companies can provide you with wonderful success stories about their distributors. It would seem that fulltimers have a great opportunity to meet new people wherever they go, greatly increasing their downlines. Someone has to be making money in this field. Why shouldn't it be you?

Bartending

Bartenders are always in demand. If you know how to mix drinks and enjoy people, you can find work at taverns, restaurants and hotels, as well as working wedding receptions and other special events. You can find job assignments through temporary work agencies or by visiting drinking establishments in person.

Christmas Tree Sales

I spent quite a bit of time talking to a couple one evening during the holiday season who were fulltimers living in a 30 foot fifth wheel. They were working at a Christmas tree sales lot and reported that the seasonal job was working out wonderfully. They received an hourly wage, and were allowed to park their RV on the lot and live in it for the duration of the selling season. Prior to that, they had sold Halloween pumpkins on another lot. Cultivate a good working relationship with a Christmas tree lot owner, and you may find yourself welcomed back with open arms next holiday season in the climate of your choice.

Wreathed In Profits

While we're on the subject of Christmas, let me mention the lady we met at the Escapee Club's Rainbow's End park in Livingston, Texas one Christmas season who made her spending money by creating custom holiday wreaths for her RVing friends and neighbors. During the year she collects odd bits of small driftwood, bells, and whatever else catches her artistic eye, and turns them into pieces of holiday art.

Newsletters

Forget the crudely drafted PTA newsletters your kids brought home from grade school - printed and e-mailed newsletters are big business these days! Professionals pay handsomely for newsletters that help them do their jobs better, that give them hard to find condensed information, or report on the latest news in their field. Investors rely on newsletters to point out the latest trends in the market, collectors of everything from rare coins to African parrots subscribe to newsletters covering their avocations. What subjects could you produce a newsletter on?

Tying Flies

A friend of mine who owns a sporting goods store routinely buys his inventory of fishing flies from three different men who spend their leisure time tying the little fake mosquitos, dragon flies and nymphs that lure lunker trout out of the deep. If you're a fly tier, you could sell your creations wholesale to the sporting goods stores you pass by on the road. And since many of your fellow campers are also fishermen, you can pick up some retail sales right in camp.

Mail Order

How can anyone who doesn't have a fixed address to receive mail be in the mail order business? Easy! There are plenty of commercial mail receiving firms that will accept your mail for you and forward the orders. You shouldn't have any trouble making arrangements for them to drop ship your customers' orders to them for a small fee. Everything from vitamins to books is sold through mail order these days. And don't overlook the great marketing potential the Internet has for your products.

Selling Ad Place Mats

One enterprising entrepreneur of my acquaintance makes an excellent living in a unique publishing endeavor. He sells advertising, which is reproduced on 11x17 inch place mats that he then distributes free to area restaurants. How's business? His place mats are filled with advertising on both sides and people are waiting in line for the next available ad space. The restaurants love this because they get free place mats instead of having to purchase them, the advertisers love the exposure, and the diners enjoy having something to read besides the same old tattoos while they're waiting for their dinner to arrive.

Liquid Assets

Retail stores, manufacturers, and wholesale companies often have excess or outdated merchandise they need to move out, and will take pennies on the dollar to free up floor space. A liquidator is one who puts sellers of this distressed merchandise together with buyers eager to take advantage of the savings, either for a straight fee or for a percentage. Other liquidators actually purchase the merchandise and resell it themselves. You can make a nice profit on these transactions, if you research your market and make yourself known to those who have something to sell and those who need it.

Fund Raising

Churches, schools, and other non-profit organizations are always looking for ways to make money. Many rely on professional fund raisers, who bring in different programs to help them, all for a fee or percentage. Fund raisers may help the group organize to sell candy bars or magazine subscriptions door to door, hold raffles, create a printed brochure or program book with paid advertising, publish a cookbook, or...? The list goes on and on, and so do the profits you can make.

Card Sharks

Legalized gambling has made a lot of people wealthy, but few of those reaping the profits are the suckers plunking down their money on blackjack tables or feeding coins into slot machines. The casinos of Las Vegas, Reno, and Laughlin, Nevada, plus a lot of other gambling meccas, hire a lot of card dealers, as well as other help, during their busy periods. There are actually schools that will teach you the fine art of dealing.

We know a couple who spend their winter parked in their RV along the Colorado River near Laughlin, working in a casino. Between wages and tips, they make enough money during a few months of the year to travel and play the rest of the time. If you don't think manipulating cards is something you can do, the same casinos also hire security guards, maintenance workers, hotel maids, and have a lot of other jobs to fill.

Don't Deal Cards, Read Them

So you don't think you're the gambling type? Maybe you can make a living reading cards instead of dealing them. Psychics can make a good living reading cards and palms, and giving readings. It's a bit offbeat, but there are those who claim to have psychic abilities, and make a living at it. Of course, if you're a psychic, do you really need this book? Can't you just read my mind for the information?

Swing Your Partner

Square dancing is very popular with the RV crowd, and there are many RVers who plan their entire trips around square dancing events. If you can call square dances, or learn to, you can tap your toes all the way to the bank.

House Sitting

House sit? Sure, why not? You can take a break from

the road, have time to do maintenance on your RV and save a lot of money in campground fees and travel expenses when you park your RV in someone's driveway and housesit for them while they're out of town. Usually all they ask is that you look after the place, maybe water the plants or feed their pets, and collect the mail. Not only will you be saving money, but the happy homeowner will pay you while you're doing it.

Installing CB Radios And Stereos

CB radios and good stereo systems are musts for anyone who spends a lot of time on the road. Installing them is simple if you know what you're doing, but can turn into a real chore for the inexperienced. If you can do a professional installation job, there's money to be made in this line. And since you're installing them anyway, why not carry a line of stereos and CBs to sell too?

Window Tinting

Don't you just hate it when that afternoon sun blasts through your side window as you drive down a desert highway? So do other RVers. With a few basic tools, some skill and a few rolls of window tinting film, you can make everyone's trip a little more comfortable, and yourself a little more affluent in the process.

Out On A Limb Of The Family Tree

My Daddy once told me I was found in the turnip patch, but later research proved that I actually come from a long line of horse thieves, con men, and shady ladies. My dog has a better pedigree than I do. Sure, we've all got some bent branches in our family trees, but we all secretly think we might just be descended from royalty. The Internet makes genealogical research fun, interesting, and much easier than searching through dusty records in the basement of some courthouse. People will pay you to help them trace their roots.

Publishing Profits

The printed word has supported my family for most of my adult life. I have owned and published periodicals ranging from free shopping guides to daily and weekly newspapers, to specialty publications. Some of the biggest money to be found in publishing is found in niche markets - creating publications that target a small, specific audience.

Among these would be newspaper or magazine format visitor guides to resort communities, publications advertising specialty items for sale, from RVs to business equipment, and guides to certain types of businesses.

Desktop publishing equipment makes it easy and inexpensive for anybody to become a publisher these days. You don't have to own any printing equipment, most of these type of publications are farmed out to central printing plants.

Put your imagination to work and think about what types of niche publications you might be able to publish. How about a series of guides to antique shops in an area where you visit? Or tabloids containing the menues for area restau-rants? You can sell enough advertising in these types of publications to make a very nice profit, and return season after season to publish new editions.

I've consulted with several publishers on the startup of such operations. And yes, you can run such a business from an RV! We publish the *Gypsy Journal*, a 36 page tabloid newspaper for RVers, from our motorhome. If you decide niche publishing just might be your niche, contact us at Publishing Partners, 1400 Colorado, Suite C-16, Boulder City, Nevada 89005 and maybe we can assist you in getting started.

RV Transport

So how do you think all those RVs arrive on the dealers lots? Most of them are too big to haul in on a flatbed truck, and the RV fairy doesn't bring them while the rest of us sleep. They're usually driven to the dealer's lot from the factory. And who better to transport a brand new RV than someone who lives in one and drives it every day? This kind of work can pay off and really give you an education on RV traveling, and the pros and cons of different models of RVs.

A Scribble Here, A Scribble There, And Dollars Everywhere

You don't have to be a Mitchner or Faulkner to sell what you write. After all, I wrote this book, and my name's not Mitchner or Faulkner. All you have to do is be able to string words together in a somewhat intelligent manner. The market for freelance work, novels, travel stories, and other types of articles is huge. It takes time to master the craft, but for those who have the persistence to write, and to hang in there through all the rejection slips that are an inevitable part of the business, there are checks waiting from publishers large and small.

Be A Census Worker

Gathering information for the United States Census isn't a regular opportunity, since the Census is taken only every so many years. But if you ever have the opportunity, sign on. The Census is always short of workers. I talked with a woman who was making a very good hourly wage as she went from door to door in one town gathering vital statistics to feed into the massive government computer system to keep a battalion of bureaucrats gainfully employed.

Golf Pro

I've never understood the game of golf. Why would you want to hit a ball as far away from you as you can, only to chase it down and hit it again? And don't tell me about all the good exercise you get - I've seen those golf carts! But a lot of people just love the sport. If you're an expert (and what golfer isn't?), maybe you can pick up some extra green to pay your green fees by becoming a roving golf pro. You might even find an RV park that will swap you a free spot in return for teaching classes to their guests. Added income could come from selling new or used equipment, or consulting with new golfers in purchasing the goodies they need.

Producing Specialty Videos

A few years ago, we were visiting Morro Bay, a

Work Your Way Across The USA

delightful town on the California coast on our honeymoon. The hotel we were staying in (this was before our RVing days) had one in-house television channel that played a continuous half hour long video on the local businesses and attractions. I became fascinated with the tape, and later contacted the producer.

He shared a lot of information with me about his business. His work consisted of going around from one resort town to another producing these simple advertising supported videos, and he reported that he was making very good money at it. Another videographer I met wanders around the country making travel videos, which he markets through a catalogue and on the Internet.

Have you always wanted to be in the movies? Well, this may be as close as you will ever get, but what the heck, you get to see a lot of neat places, and make a buck or two in the process.

Work Your Way Across The USA

Chapter 10

The Amazing World Of E-Commerce

I have to admit that even though I work with computers every day, until recently I was pretty ignorant of the potential for e-commerce - business conducted over the Internet. Sure, I knew there were a lot of businesses out there who had turned to the World Wide Web to increase their marketing opportunities. I had even purchased items online a time or two. And when short comments about our *Gypsy Journal* RV newspaper were posted in the RV forums on America Online and the Escapees Club web pages, we got quite a few requests for sample copies. We had even been planning to create a website for the newspaper.

But it was at a garage sale that we learned just how amazing the potential for RVers to make money on the Internet is. When my wife and I married a couple of years ago, we combined two three bedroom homes into one household. Needless to say, there was a lot of duplication of things like televisions, furniture, household goods, and the other things people tend to accumulate over the years. A lot of this surplus was given to our adult children, but even more found itself crammed into the garage and spare bedrooms, where it sat gathering dust. (Okay, it didn't gather dust. My wife is a fanatic about keeping the place clean, and the only thing gathering dust around here is me. But you get the point.)

Whenever someone makes the decision to go fulltiming in an RV, one of the first considerations is what to do with all of their "stuff." You can only pawn so much off on the kids, it costs a fortune to store it, and it darn sure won't all fit into your new home on wheels. Some people choose to donate a lot to various charities, but we were too greedy for that. (We were also too poor, we needed the money.)

We held several garage sales, and were amazed at the money seemingly rational people were willing to shell out for our unwanted junk. We made several thousands of dollars, and at every sale the accumulation of things we needed to dispose of grew smaller and smaller. But one thing really surprised us - the things we considered junk and almost hauled to the dump sold faster than the good things we expected to move very quickly. People quicky pulled their money out to cart off broken yard tools, old clothing, Tupperware containers, and such; but some of the high dollar items, such as our collection of antique oil lamps, antique furniture, a nearly new Snap-On tool chest and other very desirable things just didn't move.

At our last sale, all of the typical garage sale items had been sold. We were talking to one customer when she mentioned that we should list our antique oil lamps on the Internet at an online auction site called e-Bay. She told us she routinely sold items on e-Bay and had built up a small sideline business marketing her garage sale finds.

We had heard radio ads for e-Bay, and decided to

investigate. Punching up www.ebay.com on the Internet, we connected to the e-Bay site and were amazed. Literally thousands of people were listing their own auctions and selling everything from collectibles to antiques to automobiles and real estate to business equipment.

Okay, we'll give this a try, we decided, and listed several items, ranging from the toolbox to a few antiques to a step-ladder, a vintage Corvette and a customized 1958 Chevrolet pickup truck. We had no idea what we had just let ourselves in for.

By the next day, the bids were pouring in. Bidders all over the country were perched in front of their computer screens laying down bids and trying to outdo one another. The dollar figures crept higher and higher.

By the time our first auctions finished, the toolbox we hadn't been able to get $250 for at a yard sale for sold for $490. An antique oak buffet went for $500. A clothing steamer that we couldn't get $25 for at our yard sales sold for $163. Our first e-Bay auctions brought in about $2,500. The Corvette and truck didn't sell, because we had set a reserve price that had to be met, but bids climbed to $10,000, and for weeks after the auction ended, we received e-mail queries about the vehicles. We knew we were onto something.

There are several online auctions sites, but e-Bay is the granddaddy of all of them, and is doing a huge volume of business. Every month they receive 1.5 billion visitors. At any given time there are literally thousands of auctions being held in some 1600 categories, ranging from antiques to collectibles to musical instruments to computer equipment to music videos.

Work Your Way Across The USA

Since getting involved selling items on e-Bay, I've talked to several sellers who have built up part and even fulltime businesses, and are doing quite well, thank you. Here's one example of the potential from online auctions - the couple who purchased our clothing steamer live in Sedona, Arizona. Sedona is a very upscale part of the world, where real estate prices tower higher than the red rock for-mations that make the area so unique.

This young couple began going around to garage sales and purchasing items to resell on e-Bay, hoping to supplement their income enough to help with their mortgage payment. Before long they were making enough money to pay the entire mortgage and their car payment. The wife writes software programs for one of the major computer companies, and she told us it won't be long before she quits her job, because they just can't keep up with all of the business they're doing online. A school teacher acquaintance of ours began selling old fishing equipment on e-Bay over the summer break. By the time school was back in session, he was making more in Internet sales than his regular salary.

The potential for RVers to make money with e-Bay or any of the other online auction sites is tremendous. As we travel around the country, we have the opportunity to shop for collectibles, sporting goods, or whatever piques our interest. Then we can list our items at auction and (if we've bought right) make a nice profit.

There are some challenges for RVers who want to sell online, the largest being having access to a telephone line to list auction items and check up on our auctions while they run. When you have several auctions going on at the same time, you can expect to get several e-mail inquiries every day from bidders with questions about the items you're selling. If you're in a campground that offers modem access, this can be handled without too much trouble. But if you're on the road, it may be a little harder to accomplish.

For us, the solution is to accumulate enough for an auction, anywhere from ten to fifty items, then park someplace where we can connect to a telephone line for a while and place our items on the auction site. This is the most time consuming chore, though there are software options out there that will allow you to list your items offline, then download them fairly quickly. We use a program called Mr. Lister, and it is a real time saver.

eBay auctions can run from three to ten days, though most successful sellers seem to schedule seven day auctions. If an RVer were to get heavily into e-Bay, it might work out best to spend part of your time gathering items to sell, then stay in one place where you have good telephone access to conduct your auctions.

When we began fulltiming, we had several income-generating ideas we planned to pursue, including going to gun shows to sell handgun grips and accessories. We quickly learned that with eBay we could get more money for our grips without the cost of traveling to a gun show, renting tables, staying at a local RV park, and being tied down for the hours the show was open.

We know of at least one RVing couple that do not even collect merchandise, yet make a nice profit selling on eBay. They pick a small town they like and visit local antique shops, offering to sell items for the stores' owners on consignment on eBay. They report they do very well, and don't have the overhead of searching for and buying merchandise.

So what do you think you might want to sell? Antiques? Collectibles? Old sporting goods? Baseball cards? Electronics? Photography equipment? I'm convinced that anyone who uses a little bit of creativity and is willing to invest the time and money to get out and shop for bargains to resell can make very good money on e-Bay or one of the other Internet auction sites. There are several good books available on selling on eBay, check them out at your local bookstore.

Other Online Money Making Ideas

eBay isn't the only way to make money on the Internet. The world of online commerce is growing at a tremendous rate, and there are more ways to make money in cyberspace than you or I can imagine. It is quickly replacing traditional mail order for many shoppers, and any product that can be sold though mail order (and not much can't) can be successfully sold on the Internet.

Subscription sales of our *Gypsy Journal* RV newspaper, as well as our sales of back issues, books, and other related products, already strong, took a tremendous leap when we began our website at www.gypsyjournal.net, and have helped introduce the newspaper to an even wider audience. If you have a product or service, you would do well to consider creating your own website. Software programs such as FrontPage make it easy even for a non-computer nerd like myself to produce a halfway decent web page.

An attorney friend of mine in Arizona has drawn new business to her law practice by adding a website called Ask

Work Your Way Across The USA

A Lawyer, where she provides simple online consultations for a small fee. Another fellow I know has done very well selling out-of-print and hard to find books online with a simple web page. Think about what product or service you can sell online.

You don't even have to sell a product to make online profits. You can make money with a website simply by referring Web surfers to other websites! This is called an affiliate program. By adding links to other businesses, you receive a commission every time someone clicks from your website to an affiliated site and makes a purchase. One of the biggest nationwide affiliate programs is Commission Junction (www.cj.com), where you can find thousands of links to add to your website and start making money. The Internet is working for you 24 hours a day, 7 days a week, marketing your product or service.

E-zine Economics

One popular online money making opportunity is publishing e-zines, online magazines. Anybody who spends any time on the Internet will soon discover a multitude of e-zines on any topic from computers to rock climbing to building log cabins. Just like conventional publishers, e-zine publishers make money from advertising, as well as selling related products, and through affiliate programs that pay them when a reader clicks through to another website from theirs and makes a purchase. Is there a hobby, lifestyle, or topic of interest that you might enjoy publishing an e-zine about?

Work Your Way Across The USA

Chapter 11

Saving Money Is
Like Making Money

Just as important, perhaps even more important, than knowing how to make money is knowing how to save money. It's simple - the less you spend, the less you have to make. You've already learned that fulltimers usually spend much less than people living in houses and apartments, because they have less room to store things.

That doesn't mean that we have to go without or sacrifice our standard of living. On the contrary, we get to see and do things that the rest of the country never experiences. While the poor working stiffs have to cram all of their sightseeing into a week or two every summer, trying to see and do it all, and returning home exhausted from their vacation, fulltimers have the time to explore at leisure. While working people have to settle for a day at such attractions as Sea World or Disneyland before they rush off to the next destination, fulltimers have all the time in the world to really get to know theme parks and other fun places, and can often take advantage of multiple-use discounts to visit again and again.

While a few days camped beside a pristine mountain lake or rushing stream may be all that the rest of the world can squeeze into their busy schedules, fulltimers are at leisure to find a beautiful spot they like, pull up a chunk of real estate, and stay as long as they wish. Schedule? What schedule?

Cutting Corners Without Going Without

There are many ways to cut corners and save money without having to live like a pauper. Most require only a bit of thought and are pretty simple. Many times we've heard that the people with the most money are the most frugal about spending it. Did you ever stop to think that maybe that's why they have all that money?

Remember, every nickel you don't spend is a nickel you don't have to earn. As a self-made millionaire once advised me, take care of the nickels and the dollars will take care of themselves.

Just a few examples:

Do you enjoy a morning newspaper? Do you realize that that quarter or fifty cents you plunk down on the counter every morning can add up to a hundred bucks a year or more?

As an old newspaperman, I love newspapers. Not just the big city multi-edition papers, but those small town rags that list the school lunch menu, tell you who is in the hospital recovering from gall bladder surgery, and which Boy Scouts just made the rank of Eagle.

I still get my daily dose of reading, I just do it for free, now. Most campgrounds have the morning newspaper in the office, and you can browse it for free. You can always find a paper in the local library, or in many restaurants. We *do* try to buy a Sunday newspaper occasionally to take advantage of the coupons inserted inside.

Work Your Way Across The USA

Shop carefully. Use coupons, but use them wisely. My wife is a wonderful cook and loves having a stock of ingredients on hand to whip up whatever culinary creation comes to mind. But she's come to realize that often when she buys coupon items, she's forced to purchase more than she needs or can store in the small confines of our RV.

Look for bargains and specials. Many times the off-brand item is much cheaper than the brand name, and tastes just as good. Many RVers make it a point to do their grocery shopping at discount supermarkets that specialize in scratch and dent closeouts.

Only buy from the campground store in an emergency. You can expect to pay half or more over what the same item will cost you in the local grocery. Convenience costs $$$.

As you travel, get off the main highways and cruise the back roads. It's a great way to see America, and you'll stumble across lots of farmer's roadside produce stands where you can pick up some fantastic bargains.

Look before you pump. Usually the gasoline stations closest to interstate highway off-ramps are the most expensive. By driving into town you can sometimes save two or three cents a gallon. When you consider that the gasoline tank in our RV holds 75 gallons, and that we only average a little over six miles per gallon, you can see where those few cents add up in the course of a year.

The Flying J truck stop chain is very RV friendly, and most Flying Js have a separate RV island where you will find easier access to fuel pumps for large RVs. Flying J also offers a free discount card for RVers that gives us a penny a gallon off on fuel purchases, and five cents a gallon off propane. This can add up to very impressive savings in the

Work Your Way Across The USA

course of a year

We also have saved a lot of money by boondocking in Flying J parking lots across the country at night as we travel. Fulltime RVers have been called people who spend upwards of $100,000 on a motorhome or truck/trailer rig, then look for places to park for free.

Some fulltimers never boondock, while others spend weeks or even months every year parked in some out of the way corner of the USA. Quartzite, Arizona and The Slabs, near Niland in southern California, are popular boondocking spots where thousands of RVers camp for extended periods of time for free. There are many other places around the country, especially in the west, where you can park your RV without paying space rent.

We usually try to find a park, truck stop or RV friendly shopping center or store where we can spend the night for free when we're just traveling from one place to another. I just cannot justify spending $20 or more for a site in an RV park, if all we are going to do is sleep overnight and get right back on the road the next morning.

Our motorhome is self-contained, with a generator, battery bank, solar panel, and water holding tanks. This self-containment allows us to spend several days at a time without hookups. When you consider that the average cost of an RV park site is somewhere around $22 with taxes, you can quickly see where just four or five nights a month spent boondocking can really save money.

Many small towns have public parks where RVs are allowed to park overnight for free. By taking advantage of free and low cost camping opportunities, we average about $5 a night in camping costs. For a listing of over 500 places where you can camp overnight for free, see the information on our Free Camping guide in the back of this book.

Decide if you really need something, or just want it. Our RV has a satellite dish on the roof, and back in our former life I enjoyed having all of those channels to surf. But I've found that the hassle of cranking up the dish and trying to tune in a satellite at every new location is sometimes more trouble than it's worth. More times than not we can get a signal on the regular roof mounted television antenna to draw in the local stations. This gives us a better chance to know what's going on locally anyway.

Many times you'll learn about a local festival or event that you'd have never known about if you were watching some channel beamed in by satellite from across the country. More and more RV parks are offering cable television hookups to give viewers more choices. I decided to cancel my satellite service and save myself $600 a year. What can you eliminate in favor of cutting expenses? A good rule of thumb is when something new comes in the RV, something else must go to make room for it.

Slow down. Before I hit the road, I owned a Corvette. Does that tell you something about how much I like to drive fast? But driving fast costs a lot more than driving at a leisurely pace. Big motorhomes and trailers were not designed for high speed travel. I get much better gas mileage at 55 miles per hour than I do at 65. Stay in the right lane and let the rest of the world rush on by. You will save money, as well as wear and tear on your rig, and see a lot more of the country in the process.

Stay put. Traveling costs money. Instead of staying just one night in an area, stay for a week or so when you come

Work Your Way Across The USA

across a place you like. You'll get a cheaper rate from the RV park for a week's stay, and if you're not moving you're not buying fuel. Besides, you'll have a better chance to get to know an area if you take the time to search out the neat little places off the main roads.

Don't be a clothes horse. Fulltimers find that they need a much smaller wardrobe. The lifestyle is casual - jeans, shorts, tee-shirts and sweatshirts are acceptable for most occasions. And since we are free to follow the sun, we don't spend much time in really cold weather, which means we do not need a lot of winter clothing.

Take advantage of freebies. Attractions such as Disney-land are great to see, but they are also very expensive. There are lots of neat places to see across this big land of ours that don't cost anything at all. Small town museums, free band concerts in parks, nature trails.... you will find there just aren't enough hours in a day to see and do it all.

Look for discounts. Golden Age Passports and other discount passes offered by the National Park Service and state parks departments can save you a lot of money over the course of your travels. Look for every discount you can find and take advantage of them. If you're over age 55, you'll be able to get discounts at many attractions, restaurants and other businesses who appreciate mature customers.

Camp wisely. Those fancy five star resorts with their hot tubs, swimming pools, game rooms and organized activities are a lot of fun, but remember, someone has to pay for all those amenities. Guess who? And do you really use these extras you are paying extra for?

Work Your Way Across The USA

There are lots of ways to save money when you camp. Join Coast to Coast and Resorts Parks International (RPI) and your camping costs can be as low as $5 or $6 a night for full service parks. Be careful when shopping for a home park though, some memberships can cost several thousands of dollars, while others are only a few hundred bucks.

The resale market for campground memberships is strong, and you can save a small fortune by buying wisely. Escapees RV Club also has several parks where members can stay for just a few dollars a night.

There are other programs where members can camp at RV parks across the country for half the regular price. We use Passport America, and have saved a lot of money with our $44 annual member-ship. Membership in Passport America gets you access to over 700 RV parks nationwide where you can stay for half price. I recommend it to anyone.

Boondock. Boondocking, or dry camping, can mean anything from camping for free on Bureau of Land Management land in the west for weeks at a time, to simply finding an unused corner of a truck stop parking lot for the night.

Newer isn't always better, but it *is* always more expensive. Americans are conditioned to want the newest and best. Madison Avenue has convinced us that we're somehow less if we don't drive the latest car, wear the latest style and keep up with the Joneses. Be willing to settle for your old faithful car, have enough confidence to be yourself, not who the television commercials tell you to be. Then get in your old clunker and laugh all the way to the bank.

Work Your Way Across The USA

Duplication is costly. What do you already have that can do the job of something you might need to buy? Tools and housewares are good examples of this. Tupperware style containers can be used for storage of other small items when not used for saving food. One big mixing bowl can also be used for smaller batches of whatever you're whipping up. A multi-head screwdriver can take the place of several different size tools. The same for crescent wrenches. Don't spend money on something if you already have something that will do the job satisfactorily. Besides saving money on the purchase, you'll cut down on weight, which will in turn increase your fuel economy.

A good rule of thumb many fulltimers follow is that whenever anything new goes into the motorhome, something else must come out.

Bookworm? My wife and I both enjoy reading, but we've found the high costs of books, even paperbacks, can really add up. And all that weight is just too much to haul around the country.

We save a lot of money by trading the books we've read to used bookstores for new (to us) reading material. Many times the RV parks we stop at also have book exchanges. Local libraries usually won't allow travelers to check out books, but you can spend a pleasant afternoon reading magazines and browsing through the books in the library, and it doesn't cost a penny.

Take advantage of your loose schedule. Often movie theaters have an afternoon matinee for half price. Since you don't have to be tied to a job during the day, take advantage of these money saving offers. But try to avoid buying sodas, popcorn, or candy. Movie theaters subsidize their operation with the high costs of these goodies.

Many restaurants also offer Early Bird specials to help build business during their slow mid-to-late afternoon hours. Dining out almost always costs more than eating at home. But if you *are* going to dine out, eat early and save!

Free entertainment. Free is a word every RVer loves the sound of. As you travel, seek out free entertainment. High school band concerts and football games. Presentations at the local library or community college. Entertainment sponsored by your RV park. Did you ever spend an hour or two watching a softball game in the park, or a small town Fourth of July parade? There's plenty to see and do without reaching for your wallet. Always remember, saving money is like making money.

Work Your Way Across The USA

Chapter 12

You Can Do It Too!

By now you've seen just how easy it is to make money on the road. You may even be asking yourself why you waited so long to take the plunge if it is this easy. Don't ask me, I still don't know why I waited so long, so how do you expect me to figure out all of your little neurosis too?

Which business or money making plan is right for you? Only you can decide that. Or you may want to do as my wife and I do and combine two or three or more ideas to give you some diversity as you travel. This is what our friends Joe and Vicki Kieva, who conduct RV lifestyle seminars across the country, call the Little Bit method of earning money - you make a little bit here and a little bit there, doing a little bit of this and a little bit of that. Our plans call for some desktop publishing, some writing, some online auction sales, a little gun show vending, a bit of consulting, and for repairing the occasional windshield. We know that in every area of the country we visit, there are at least one or two ways for us to make money. And if we do find the pickings slim in one region, we can just roll up the awning, unplug the water and power connections and head on down the road to a better location. That's the great things about this lifestyle - the freedom to choose.

Work Your Way Across The USA

You have the ability to go wherever you want, whenever you want. If you like the fast pace of a major metropolitan area, there is no shortage of ways to earn a living. If you prefer the serenity of small town life, you're free to find your own little Mayberry and settle down for a week, a month or even longer. You are truly in charge of your own destiny.

You might want to work swap meets on the weekends, and scrub a few windows clean midweek. Or maybe teach a class or two in the evenings at your favorite RV resort. One thing's for certain, you'll never get bored - there's a new town and a new adventure waiting just over the next hill. Good luck, and happy traveling.

Appendix

Free And Low Cost Camping Resources

Don Wright's Guide to Free Campgrounds, Eastern Edition Lists thousands of free and low cost (under $12) campgrounds in the eastern half of the United States. $18.95 plus shipping. Available from Cottage Publications, 800-272-5518 or from Cottage Publications (www.cottagepub.com)

Don Wright's Guide to Free Campgrounds, Western Edition Lists thousands of free and low cost (under $12) campgrounds in the western half of the United States. $18.95 plus shipping. Available from Cottage Publications, 800-272-5518 or from Cottage Publications (www.cottagepub.com)

Camping With The Corps of Engineers – Excellent guidebook to over 900 COE campgrounds nationwide. $13.95 plus shipping. Available from Cottage Publications, 800-272-5518 or from Cottage Publications (www.cottagepub.com)

Passport America – Members pay an annual fee of $49 and receive a 50% discount at over 900 campgrounds nationwide. 800-283-7183 (www.campsave50percent.com).

Recreation USA Camping Club – Members pay an annual

fee of $99 and have access to hundreds of campgrounds nationwide for $10 a night. 850-537-9641 (www.campingandcampgrounds.com)

RV Clubs

Escapees RV Club – This is what we feel is the best organization for fulltime and extended travel RVers, or any other traveler. The club's many benefits and services include several Escapees owned RV parks and co-ops that offer low cost camping, discounts at hundreds of RV parks nationwide, bi-monthly magazine, telephone calling card, an excellent mail forwarding service, two big rallies every year, numerous smaller events, and much more. 888-757-2582 (www.escapees.com)

Good Sam Club – Over one million RVing families belong to the Good Sam Club. Member benefits include 10% discounts at over 1,700 RV parks nationwide, monthly magazine, free trip routing, roadside service plans, mail forwarding services, rallies and more. 800-234-3450. (www.goodsamclub.com)

Family Campers & RVers – Nationwide RV club with an emphasis on family-oriented activities. Membership benefits include a magazine, rallies, camping discounts, and more. (www.fcrv.org)

FMCA – Family Motor Coach Association membership is open to motorhome owners only, no travel trailers or fifth wheels. The club has dozens of rallies large and small across the country, a full color monthly magazine, roadside service plans, and more. 800-543-3622 (www.fmca.com)

Working On The Road

Workamper News – Excellent bi-monthly publication and web site listing job opportunities for RVers and Situation Wanted advertisements from RVers looking for work, and profiles of working RVers. (501) 362-2637 (www.workamper.com)

Workers on Wheels – Great website listing jobs available for RVers. (www.wow.com)

Support Your RV Lifestyle – Jaimie Hall has written *the* definitive book for working RVers, listing types of jobs available, resources for finding work with private employers, and in state and federal parks. This is the one book *working* RVers must have. $19.95 plus $3.50 shipping Available from Pine Country Publishing, 127 Rainbow Drive #2780, Livingston, Texas 77399-1027. E-mail CalamityJaimie@escapees.com

Work Your Way Across The USA – Based on Nick Russell's popular seminars by the same name presented at RV events across the country, this book explores ways RVers can make a part or fulltime income with jobs they can do from the road, and small businesses that can be operated from an RV.

Work Your Way Across The USA

$12.95 plus $3.50 shipping. Available from Gypsy Journal, 1400 Colorado St. #C-16, Boulder City, Nevada 89005. (www.gypsyjournal.net)

Books Of Interest To RVers

Watch It Made in the U.S.A. – An excellent guide to factory tours all across the country, with address and contact information. Available from Avalon Travel Publishing (www.factorytour.com)

RV Repair and Maintenance Manual – Bob Livingston's excellent guide to taking care of your RV and handling many repairs yourself instead of going to a service center. This book will save you hundreds of dollars. This is a must-have for every RV bookshelf. $34.95 plus shipping. Published by Trailer Life Books.

Work Your Way Across The USA

Come Along For The Ride!

Life on the road as fulltime RVers is always an adventure, and you can be a part of it! Subscribe to the *Gypsy Journal* today and ride along with our two modern day ramblers as they explore America's highways and back roads, introducing you to small town museums, little known attractions, historical sites, and the weird, wacky, and wonderful people they meet along the way. Just $15 for one year or $25 for two years brings you all the fun! (Canadian subscriptions, please add $5 and make payment in US dollars.) All subscriptions delivered by first class mail to insure forwarding for our traveling readers.

More Great Reading From The Gypsy Journal!

RVers Dashboard Companion – This must have guidebook lists every Wal-Mart, Sam's Club, Flying J, and Cracker Barrel in the country, with driving directions, telephone number, and GPS coordinates. $24.95 plus $3.75 shipping. To order, send check or money order to Gypsy Journal, 1400 Colorado #C-16, Boulder City, Nevada 89005 or order online by logging onto www.PayPal.com and making payment with your credit card to BookOrders@gypsyjournal.net.

Gypsy Journal's Guide To Free Campgrounds & Overnight Parking Spots - Save hundreds of dollars as you travel with this great listing of over 500 city and county parks, businesses, and public lands where you can camp for free! Many include either full or partial hookup sites. $8.95 postpaid. To order, send check or money order to Gypsy Journal, 1400 Colorado #C-16, Boulder City, Nevada 89005 or order online by logging onto www.PayPal.com and making

Work Your Way Across The USA

payment with your credit card to BookOrders@gypsyjournal.net.

RVers Guide To Fairgrounds Camping - Most RVers never realize how many great, money saving camping opportunities fairgrounds have to offer. This guide to over 250 fairgrounds nationwide is a must for every budget conscious RV owner. $7.50 postpaid. To order, send check or money order to Gypsy Journal, 1400 Colorado #C-16, Boulder City, Nevada 89005 or order online by logging onto www.PayPal.com and making payment with your credit card to BookOrders@ gypsyjournal.net.

RVers Guide To Casino Parking - Casinos. They're not just for gambling anymore. Many casinos offer RVers free or low cost overnight parking opportunities from coast to coast. This guide lists RV-friendly casinos from across the country where you will find a safe place to park for free or at low cost, and enjoy a good meal along with an evening's entertainment as well, if you need to unwind from a hard day on the road. $6.95 postpaid. To order, send check or money order to Gypsy Journal, 1400 Colorado #C-16, Boulder City, Nevada 89005 or order online by logging onto www.PayPal.com and making payment with your credit card to BookOrders@ gypsyjournal.net.

Overnight Parking With The VFW - Many VFW Posts welcome traveling veterans who belong to other Posts to pull off the road and spend the night in their parking lots. Some even offer RV hookups! Most Posts do not charge their fellow veterans for this courtesy, and those who do ask only a token fee. This booklet lists VFW Posts around the nation that welcome you for a visit. Reap one of the benefits

Work Your Way Across The USA

of your service to your country and your VFW membership. $5.50 postpaid. To order, send check or money order to Gypsy Journal, 1400 Colorado #C-16, Boulder City, Nevada 89005 or order online by logging onto www.PayPal.com and making payment with your credit card to BookOrders@ gypsyjournal.net. *VFW parking is available to members of the Veterans of Foreign Wars only.*

Gypsy Journal's Guide to Public RV Dump Stations - A must-have for every traveling RVer and boondocker, this great booklet lists nearly 1,000 RV dump stations from coast to coast and in Canada too. $7.50 postpaid. To order, send check or money order to Gypsy Journal, 1400 Colorado #C-16, Boulder City, Nevada 89005 or order online by logging onto www.PayPal.com and making payment with your credit card to BookOrders@gypsyjournal.net.

Meandering Down The Highway – A collection of travelogues from the *Gypsy Journal* RV travel newspaper, this book follows workaholic baby boomers Nick and Terry Russell as they make the switch to the RV lifestyle, trading long hours, stress, and a houseful of "stuff" for a simpler life on the road. $16.95 plus $3.50 shipping. To order, send check or money order to Gypsy Journal, 1400 Colorado #C-16, Boulder City, Nevada 89005 or order online by logging onto www.PayPal.com and making payment with your credit card to BookOrders@gypsyjournal.net.

LaVergne, TN USA
23 June 2010
187119LV00004B/12/A